BABES IN THE BIGHOUSE

*Book and Lyrics by
Megan Terry
Structure by
Jo Ann Schmidman
Music by John J Sheehan*

BROADWAY PLAY PUBLISHING INC
New York
www.broadwayplaypublishing.com
info@broadwayplaypublishing.com

Cover photo by Megan Terry

First published by B P P I in *Plays By Megan Terry* in December 2000
This edition: December 2017
I S B N: 978-0-88145-720-9

Book design: Marie Donovan
Page make-up: Adobe Indesign
Typeface: Palatino

BABES IN THE BIGHOUSE (A Documentary Fantasy
About Life in a Women's Prison) was first presented
at the Omaha Magic Theatre, Omaha, Nebraska,
on 15 November 1974. It then toured the U S, in
O M T's repertory for the next three years. The
following appeared in BABES at various times:

Jill Anderson

Carol Dietz

Joe Guinan

Judith Katz

Jim Laferla

James Larson

Nancy Larson

Michael Malstead

Jo Ann Schmidman

Rae Ann Schmitz

Elisa Stacy

Mary Thatcher

Stephanie Toothacher

Kate Ullman

Donna Young

Director .... JoAnn Schmidman
Score composed and played by .... John J Sheehan
Song: Pardon Me *composed by* .... Jill Anderson
Set design .... Megan Terry & JoAnn Schmidman
Light design .... Judy Gillespie & Colbert McClellan
Net design one .... Mitza Thompson
Net design two ....Diane Degan

ENVIRONMENT

For the Omaha Magic Theatre production the playing area was a rectangular shape ten feet by forty feet. This was dictated by the shape of our building. There were two to three rows of raised seating for the audience along the forty foot sides. Double-decker cells for the inmates were constructed of metal scaffolding *(which we painted bright yellows, reds, blues and greens)* at one end of the playing area. At the O M T the cells were at the entrance to the theater. The audience, upon entering and buying tickets, were immediately confronted with the cells, each individually outlined with seven-watt Christmas tree lights. The small corridor leading to the seating area was roped off so that the audience was confined in the lobby.

While the audience waits, an audiotape plays. We made our tape by going door-to-door and asking people on the street questions about what they think goes on inside a women's prison. We found that the majority of responses were influenced by the gross amount of cheap sex novels, "grade C" drive-in movies and personal fantasies, all having to do with women locked up, as punishment, together. Therefore, the actors at O M T were dressed in various combinations of corsets, long gloves, feathers and furs, garters, fishnet hose, spike heels and too much makeup.

Opposite the cells at the other end of the playing area is a six-inch-high platform (five feet by six feet).

A net hangs from the ceiling grazing the length of the platform. The net at O M T was made from an old volleyball net. Affixed to the net were crocheted aprons, doilies and other articles which the prisoners made in crafts class. There is a 3′ opening slit in the center of the net.

At various times in the play, the platform is used as the warden's office, the doctor's office and solitary confinement ("The Hole").

The area between the platform and the cells represents at various times—hallways, the shower room, the yard and the sewing room. The dominant dramatic image in the play is "how the women walk." They walk the halls from cells to laundry to cafeteria, etc.

As the actors/inmates walk through the hall, they focus their attention on the rhythms inside their heads.

The interior rhythms should be projected outward in the way each individual walks. Each actor selects many characters to play throughout the evening and this will be evident in the transformation of the walks.

NOTE: Reasons for "the interior" are to maintain sanity, to withdraw from others, to space out, to state who they are, etc, or to show dominance or confusion as a guard. When actors aren't involved in a scene with dialogue, at the director's discretion they may continue the "walks."

The other dominant dramatic image in the play is the "imposing of wills." Inmates impose wills on one another and on the guards. Several weeks of workshop were spent working on "the wills." We discovered when one imposed her will on another, the object of the will imposition resisted. This created tension—a push/pull situation—and the image was momentarily frozen until a guard came upon them, an inmate approached or a prison noise would startle them.

(These may be actual or imagined.) This caused those involved in the imposing of wills to pull away, change their focus, break the tension and thus change the image, returning to "the walks." O M T never performs BABES in proscenium. When we tour to a proscenium theater, we have all the audience seated on stage, in rows of seats facing each other along the longest side of the stage (on a deep, narrow stage, along the left and right of the playing area; on a wide, shallow stage, along the front and back). No one sits in the "house". This does limit seating, but maintains the feeling of the audience as observers inside a prison.

COSTUMES

For Opening Section: The actors are dressed in the most extreme of the audience's fantasies of how "bad girls" look. At the O M T we used cheap prison novels, the covers of *True Detective* magazines and grade C women's prison movies as prime resources.

For the Body of the Play: The women prisoners were dressed in the simplest cotton housedresses and tennis shoes. When they transform into guards they slip on colorful band uniform jackets. When they transform into the visiting evangelists, they don thrift-shop fashions and "proper" ladies' hats.

dedicated to the women and men in prison in the
U S and Canada who asked us to make this play and to
John J Sheehan, Composer, Conductor, Performer

ACT ONE

*(The play begins. All twinkle lights twinkle up, as do
playing area lights. The audio tape is turned off. The actors
enter in extreme slow motion. They flirt with, seduce and
try every available means to con the spectators. Gradually
the audience members become aware of the actors who move
toward them. They can only view the actors through the jail
cells. Because of the physical setup, the audience has to work
to see what is going on. As the actors enter their cells, the
slow motion ends and each begins her opening monologue to
con. Each actor speaks directly to various audience members
trying to convince each one of her innocence.)*

(When JOCKEY *begins to speak to the audience, twinkle
lights on all cells remain on. Those lights on her cell flash
in rhythm to her speech. When she takes focus, general light
comes up on all cells.)*

JOCKEY: Listen! You aren't gonna see what really
goes on here. They'll have the whole place—and
us—sanitized, de-loused, sterile, perfect and old-time
Christian clean. They'll make you very happy with
the way your tax dollars are being spent. Their lives
depend on that, you bet! But make them show you
the hole. They got a hole in here—they call it "The
Adjustment Center." They want everything here to
sound like a hospital or a school so you'll think that
with a new name somethin's changed around here.
No matter how many times they call it a "campus,"

this place is still a joint. You know what happens here? Nothing. Nothing. And then lots more of the same. They taught me how to fill a bucket with water and soap. Where to put my hands on the handle of a mop and how to tell the floor from the walls. When I get out of here, I get to be the best hotel maid in the world—but I'm allergic to detergent. Look at my hands—all the skin is peeling off.

*(The lights continue to twinkle—*JOCKEY *and* RONNIE *are cellmates.)*

RONNIE: Hi. How're you tonight? Welcome to our "campus." It's such a nice drive on a clear day. I get into town often lately. Some groups who're interested in us ask for me to come and speak to them about how we're doing here. And believe me, I'm glad to talk about it. I've come a long way since I got convinced I was my own worst enemy. I was doing hard time. I was so mean I spent forty-nine days in the "Adjustment Center." I wasn't about to change for nobody. But then it dawned on me that the more I stayed in a negative vibration state, the longer it would be till I could get back out into the free world. I just had to turn myself around and become the other side of the coin. For the first six months I had nothing but all the shit jobs—scrubbing and scrubbing and then rubbing. When it got dry they let me paint it—you know what I mean? But now I've worked my way up to be head clerk of records here. I'm saving my money. I got a bank account. I'm getting skills I could use in an insurance company or any nice, clean business like that. Now I'm doing easy time and looking forward to joining you all one day soon. Loan me a cigarette?

(Twinkle lights come up on CHAMP's *cell. They remain on around* RONNIE *and* JOCKEY's *cell.* RONNIE *exits to change to* MISS SCHNAUZER.*)*

CHAMP: Hello? You come with a tour group? Wanna play ball? Got a good team here. El Toro bats three-fifty, and that's on her bad days. Listen, would you ask the Warden if she'll let you take us swimming? I want to see something else. We get tired of looking at each other. You roller skate? I was All Junior Champ in high school. They gave me up to two years for possession. You believe it? Don't you think it's pretty silly to spend all your money keeping me here for two jays? My problem is I didn't think big enough... They pardon the guys, the really *big* guys. They got respect for the big guys. Us little women, they bust us and throw away the key. I was out riding in the first car I could ever afford to buy myself—had only two jays in my pocket. It was on the way to get my inspection sticker. Lucky it was my first offense or I'd have up to six. Cute, eh? Write your Congressman. I write every day. If you don't have a record, they might even take you seriously. Try it. Costs a hell of a lot of dough to keep me here. I'd rather be surf fishing in San Clemente!

(Lights twinkle around EL TORO's *cell—stay on, on* CHAMP's.*)*

EL TORO: Nobody gonna rehabilitate you! You rehabilitate yourself, y'understand? Like, if I'm sitting here and you tell me to sit a certain way and look prim and proper like a lady...I'm not gonna feel like doing that. That ain't me. I like to sit and think, and I don't smile when I'm looking inside, y'understand? Sometimes I get up in the morning, I want to take a walk. I might want to talk to someone. But they don't let you talk to anyone until after one P M on Saturday. They got me trained to wake up at six-thirty A M. *(Laughs, sputters)* I used to go to *bed* at six-thirty A M! They got me working in the sewing shop now, and I like it O K. But when I first came here they couldn't understand me. They don't realize that some of us out there, *we don't work*. Not everybody has to do a nine-to-fiver for chump change, y'understand. They write me up all the time about my attitude. The matron always is looking at me *(Demonstrates)* when I'm like this, see—sitting and tripping on myself—and she says, "What's wrong wit chew? You're not happy!" I'm perfectly happy, *sitting here*. But around here they want you always to be sitting like this *(She demonstrates a super-perfect, little girl pose.)* and grinning like an ape. Otherwise they think you've gone mental! Like this babe we had in here. She set fire to her mattress because they wouldn't let her hold hands with the person she was sweet on. They sent her to California. Told her she'd be happier there. Told her there were no girls here like the "way" she was, y'understand? But there were five hundred of them in the prison in California and she wouldn't have to set fire to her mattress there.

(Lights twinkle around KATHLEEN's *cell—remain on* EL TORO's.)

KATHLEEN: I wouldn't work in a job where they can keep track of you. You got to be out of your mind, honey. I know what I'm talking about. My poor old mama, she worked in a square job all her life. She worked as a waitress, she worked as a florist. She had a trade, honey. You know what I mean—she was an artist with flowers! When her arthritis got so bad she couldn't make corsages and funeral sprays no more, she went back into waitressing at Dunkin' Donuts. She worked all her life—like since they invented Social Security—you dig? She kept all her forms and she wrote down all her numbers, you dig? She was always up front with her numbers. So she retires two years ago. You know what the government gives her for working from the time she was ten years old—you know what they give her? Seventy-eight dollars a

month. Count 'em. Thanks a lot. Working fifty-five
years, you dig? Fifty-five years. How's she supposed
to live on seventy-eight dollars a month?? You figure it
out. She'd be better off in here with us.

*(The sound rises fully as all prisoners now join with
KATHLEEN, speaking key phrases from their speeches. All
lights twinkle until MISS SCHNAUZER, a prison official,
appears at opposite end of the playing area. When the women
see her, they fall silent and withdraw into their darkened
cells. During MISS SCHNAUZER's speech they change to
prison dresses and tennis shoes. Over their dresses they
wear identical green or blue hospital or prison gowns.
MISS SCHNAUZER wears a gray and red guard coat. [In
the Omaha Magic Theatre production, when prisoners
transformed to guards, they slipped into bright marching
band uniform jackets.] MISS SCHNAUZER unties the rope
which has kept the audience confined to the lobby. She shakes
some hands, welcoming them into the prison, and directs
them to seats. She smiles to both sides of the audience, makes
a gesture of welcome, stops, looks down at the floor. She's not
used to addressing so many people from the free world at one
time. She straightens up, works to relax her body, her eyes
showing inner disturbance. As she speaks she scans each
audience member very closely. She is checking to see that
no contraband [matches, cigarettes, a sharp object, a belt] is
brought into the prison. Years of watching for the passing of
contraband and/or the tapping of love messages on toes keep
her from letting go of the "guard" mind set. She may be any
age, but seems youthful and "with it.")*

MISS SCHNAUZER: Hello there—I'm Miss Schnauzer,
Assistant to our Warden, in charge of working with
the Parole Board, the Legislature, and you—the
community—and I want to welcome you to our
campus. I think some of you may have noticed the
new sign just to the right of the front gate: "WOMEN'S
STATE CORRECTIONAL FACILITY." The legislature

was kind enough to vote us a new name this year
and we were able to paint a new sign with materials
left over from repairing our "Adjustment Center."
In the dark ages of penology, there was a place
where inmates were confined for punishment, which
our charges referred to as "solitary confinement,"
or euphemistically, as "the hole." But since the
sociological-anthropo-sensitivity-psychiatric revolution
has brought us into this new age of enlightenment—
and thus more humane treatment geared toward
rehabilitation—what used to be called "the hole" is
now a gaily painted place where inmates who may be
feeling upset may go to meditate—alone—away from
the *hubbub* of correctional life.

*(She crosses to area in front of cells as she speaks. By this
time most of the changing activity has been completed—at
least all uncovering that the audience shouldn't see. As she
crosses, lights follow her. They go out as she passes out of the
area.)*

MISS SCHNAUZER: As East has met West, we in the
West have been wise enough at times, I hope, to gear
up and make use of some of the applicable Far Eastern
personal development techniques which can be
utilized in bringing sanity and calmness to some of our
angrier ladies.

*(Distant growls and bar rattling noise from the cell areas.
MISS SCHNAUZER waits for it to end. She does not look at
inmates but holds a smile on the audience.)*

MISS SCHNAUZER: A few days of meditation and
scientifically controlled fasting in "The Adjustment
Center" helps a disturbed individual realize she'd
rather have the company of her new friends here as
well as three square meals a day. Further, I'd like to
call your attention to the up-to-date plumbing. No
woman has to flush a toilet herself. The flushing is

controlled at the central guard station. This way one
matron can supervise an entire cottage of girls, where
it might have taken up to five before. This saves you,
our employers and taxpayers, money in eliminated
salaries. I'm really happy you were able to come today,
as tensions sometimes run high here and seeing faces
from the free world, faces of those who know how
to live on the street—I mean in ordinary society—
can an act as an inspiration to our girls. As I'm sure
you realize, by the time a girl is placed in here she's
reached rock bottom. We work hard with the girls to
help build up their self images, to teach them a trade so
they may one day take their places as useful members
of society. You'll hear various stories today. Please take
most of them with a grain of salt. A lot of our girls have
lived quite unreal lives and they do exaggerate their
cases, and the reasons why they are here. But please
understand me, we do show compassion for our girls,
but not sympathy. You may feel at times that you want
to show sympathy toward some of them, but let me
caution you in advance: "sympathy is weakness." They
won't respect you for it. They'll respect you if you
respect them, but "sympathy is weakness," and they'll
use every con game in the book to get you to fall for
their stories. Thank you again for coming and showing
an interest in what we're trying to do. We do need
more money for staff and better facilities and you can
help us toward these with your vote. And now we'll
show you a composite picture of a day in the life of our
facility. Please don't feed the inmates or ask to eat with
us. Our budget doesn't cover you.

(MISS SCHNAUZER *breaks into an enormous, toothy smile
which freezes on her face. She rotates so that all the audience
partakes of her good will. One prisoner comes out of her cell
transformed to a* GUARD *wearing a blue and red jacket. She
marches toward* MISS SCHNAUZER, *who stands smiling*

and rotating. They perform a military "changing of the guard." The new GUARD *lifts a violin to her shoulder and plays a dissonant chord to signify the prison bell. At sound of the chord, twinkle lights come up on cells and prisoners press noses to cell bars for count. Each prisoner, in an order established by the director, calls out a number from one to forty. These numbers vary from count to count.)*

JOCKEY: Two

OX TAIL: Seven.

CHAMP: Sixteen.

EL TORO: Twenty-eight.

RONNIE: Thirty-six.

KATHLEEN: Forty.

*(*GUARD *marches to cells and unlocks doors. [In Omaha Magic Theatre's production this was signified by hitting cell bars with a chain.] The prisoners [except* KATHLEEN, *who has been restricted] come out of their cells, stretching and yawning.* GUARD *moves to center playing area and mimes turning on showers. [In O M T's production the prisoners wore green surgical gowns as robes over their other costumes.] As they wait for their showers, the* GUARD *drags* KATHLEEN *from her cell and takes her to a shower way from the other women. During the following scene this* GUARD *takes a great deal of interest in* KATHLEEN's *shower. Periodically,* KATHLEEN *will catch the* GUARD *in the act of looking her up and down. The* GUARD *looks away just before their eyes meet. The other prisoners mime taking their showers [they do not remove their clothes].* RONNIE *showers with the rest, but listens and does not speak.)*

(Under the showers:)

EL TORO: Got any kids?

CHAMP: Four. You?

EL TORO: Had two, but only know where one is.

JOCKEY: I got two. What happened to the other?

EL TORO: I don't know.

CHAMP: When'd you have it?

EL TORO: Reform school. I know it was alive. Right after birth I held her just for a minute. But then they knocked me out with something, and when I came to, they told me the baby died. I still don't believe them.

CHAMP: Awww, they adopted it out, I bet.

JOCKEY: Probably sold it.

CYNTHIA: Yeah, I heard of 'em doing that.

EL TORO: I've got my Ma, and a volunteer lawyer trying to track her down. I know in my heart she's alive.

JOCKEY: You saw her alive?

EL TORO: That's how come I know she was a girl.

(She winks at CHAMP, *beckons her to join in her joke on* JOCKEY*—they both sneak up on* JOCKEY*)*

EL TORO: She was so beautiful…when she was born the doctor threw her up on my breast… *(Directly behind* JOCKEY*)* …and she went right for the nipple!

(They grab JOCKEY's *breast.)*

JOCKEY: *(Shocked, then laughing)* That's a girl all right!

(All in shower laugh. MATRON *becomes vaguely aware of the disturbance. She has been totally submerged in her action with* KATHLEEN. EL TORO *immediately acts as if she is comforting* JOCKEY, *who immediately acts as if she's ill.* CHAMP *acts normal, keeps showering as her cover.)*

MATRON: All right, keep it down—you're turnin' into prunes.

(MATRON takes KATHLEEN *from the shower [she was clearly not finished showering] and places her in solitary*

confinement behind the net. KATHLEEN *looks for a way out, finds methods of making the time pass during her stay behind "the net." The prisoners finish their showers and dress.* JOCKEY *and* EL TORO *dress, while in line with the others,* JOCKEY *in front of* EL TORO.*)*

JOCKEY: Don't get butch with me—we're not home.

EL TORO: Since when I live at yer house?

JOCKEY: Whatcha got, a hormone rush?

EL TORO: I washed my hands and I can't do a thing with 'em. *(Runs fingers up and down* JOCKEY'*s body.)*

JOCKEY: I'll have ta get butch and beat yer ass.

EL TORO: *(Bumping buns)* We could go to different holes together.

JOCKEY: Who ya been takin' butch lessons from?

EL TORO: Not from you, you bum fuck! *(Sticks out tongue)*

JOCKEY: *(Grabs tongue)* You stick that out, ya got to use it.

EL TORO: Why, Miss Butch, you flirting with me?

(The violin/bell sounds, women line up for the count. They measure an arm's length between them and begin:)

JOCKEY: Six.

RONNIE: Thirteen.

CHAMP: Fifteen.

EL TORO: Twenty-seven.

KATHLEEN: Thirty.

(The prisoners move to scrub the floor. As they scrub, RONNIE *transforms into* MATRON ONE, CYNTHIA *into* MATRON TWO. *They stand back to back—they keep watch. Their eyes dart from prisoner to prisoner, from one audience*

member to another, checking for disruptions and contraband. They move, still back to back, in a circle as they speak.)

MATRON ONE: It's a clear day.

MATRON TWO: Not a cloud.

MATRON ONE: Did you hear about Lieutenant Meeker?

MATRON TWO: What?

MATRON ONE: Totaled her car last night.

MATRON TWO: Oh, no.

MATRON ONE: Yeah, can't save it.

MATRON TWO: That car was a classic.

MATRON ONE: I always told her if she hung on to it, she'd get five thousand for it in about twenty years.

MATRON TWO: I saw an article in *Time* that they're selling old cars down in Austin for fifty to eighty thousand.

MATRON ONE: I saw that, too.

MATRON TWO: My Dad had a truck come and haul his Oldsmobile away two years ago.

MATRON ONE: The one with the fins?

MATRON TWO: That's the one.

MATRON ONE: How much is it worth now?

MATRON TWO: Aw, they squashed it into a cube and sold it for scrap, but if it was in running order, I figure Dad coulda sold it for thirty thousand in about twenty years. There wasn't a dent in it and the chrome was perfect.

MATRON ONE: No rust?

MATRON TWO: Not that I noticed.

(MATRON ONE *plays violin/belt sound. Women line up for count.)*

JOCKEY: Seven.

CHAMP: Ten.

EL TORO: Sixteen.

KATHLEEN: Twenty-eight.

MATRON TWO: Specified women report to the sewing room... *(Going down line at random)* You...you...YOU... you...

(If company size allows, MATRON TWO oversees workers in sewing room. The women who were picked move on to the sewing room where they pantomime folding and ironing sheets. As this happens, EL TORO and JOCKEY move to the net to tell KATHLEEN that they weren't able to get her the contraband [valium] they had promised her. Whispers— discussion ensues. A MATRON intervenes. If company is small, MATRON TWO transforms back into CYNTHIA for work in the sewing room.)

MATRON: No talking.

EL TORO: *(Innocent)* Just saying hello.

MATRON: You know the rules.

EL TORO: What's wrong with hello?

MATRON: Nothing. Hello, El Toro. You're elected to scrub this hall.

(Kicks her behind the knee, forcing EL TORO to the floor.)

EL TORO: But I just scrubbed it this morning.

MATRON: It's dirty from all the hellos. Every time you say hello, El Toro, you say it so juicy you get spit on my clean floor. Down on your knees.

(Notices JOCKEY still talking quietly to KATHLEEN)

MATRON: You, too. You there.

JOCKEY: Me?

MATRON: You, lady. Down and scrub.

(Hands mop to JOCKEY, *sponge and bucket to* EL TORO.)

MATRON: Learn to be a good little housekeeper and you can get a first-class man when you get out. Real good housekeepers are careful of their work.

*(Points out blemishes on floor—*JOCKEY *follows her around and scrubs.)*

MATRON: There's a spot, and there's a spot.

(Finds one in front of EL TORO.)

EL TORO: That's your shadow.

MATRON: Why, so it is.

(Kicks bucket, drenching EL TORO *with water.)*

MATRON: And my shadow just kicked the bucket. Hurry it up, don't let the water get into the cells, or you'll be mopping all week. *(Marching)* Faster, faster. No man would put up with such a slow wife, ladies. Elbow grease, that's what my Granddad said it takes— elbow grease.

(Gritting their teeth, the two women work as fast as possible to mop up the water.)

(Scene Five is the sewing room—circle of light in front of the cells. The prisoners mime folding and ironing sheets and pillowcases. Two MATRONS *are supervising.* MATRON TWO *is the instructor or overseer of the work.* MATRON ONE *has just entered. She stands in front of the net, checks out and collects the tools of the work. This scene is to be done with easy familiarity and playfulness.)*

CHAMP: Another day, another two-and-a-half cents from "Sam."

JOCKEY: *(Comes into the sewing room after scrubbing the floor)* Minus two, ya mean.

ALL: Yeah, you can say that again. I know what you mean. *(Et cetera)*

JOCKEY: Yeah, man, when I get out, I'm gonna buy a Silver Cloud Rolls Royce with all the millions I'm earning in this joint.

(EL TORO *has come in from scrubbing floors, folds sheets with* JOCKEY.)

OX TAIL: You'll be lucky if you can buy one skate.

EL TORO: Can't afford a skate key, I'm so in debt.

OX TAIL: You owe me seven cartons of cigarettes. Be rest of your life paying off.

EL TORO: Ah, c'mon baby, take it out in trade.

OX TAIL: Since ya asked me nice.

CHAMP: *(To* MATRON ONE*)* l saw the way you smiled at Mrs Snowden.

MATRON ONE: I'm feeling good today.

JOCKEY: You're always feeling good when you're near Mrs Snowden.

(The others laugh. MATRON ONE *blushes.)*

OX TAIL: Hey, look, Mrs Beecroft is blushing.

MATRON TWO: Keep it down to a dull roar. Let's get the work out, okay?

EL TORO: She's sweet on Snowden.

MATRON ONE: My husband would be interested to hear that.

CHAMP: What he don't know won't hurt him.

MATRON ONE: Okay, cut the kidding.

JOCKEY: Kidding? Who's kidding?

EL TORO: And they put us in the hole for getting married.

MATRON ONE: Come on, hurry it up or I'll have to write you up.

JOCKEY: Yer cute when yer mad.

MATRON TWO: You listen to too many movies.

OX TAIL: She don't "watch" 'em, that's for sure.

JOCKEY: Would be the waste of a good movie.

CHAMP: Hey, Mrs Beecroft, can I call you up for a date when I get out of here?

MATRON ONE: You'll never get out of here if you spend all your time on love affairs.

CHAMP: Affairs? Affairs? I'm a fine, upstanding, married Christian woman with two children.

OX TAIL: And three wives.

(They all laugh.)

EL TORO: No, she's only got two. One lucked out of here last week.

MATRON ONE: I didn't hear any crying.

CHAMP: This joint is a supermarket and all the tomatoes are free.

OX TAIL: Mrs Snowden is looking at Mrs Beecroft, now.

MATRON TWO: To signal her to write you up for distracting four people from doing their work. *(She says this with warmth.)*

OX TAIL: Yer an all-right chick, Mrs Beecroft—

MATRON ONE: Woman, not chick.

OX TAIL: That matron on the night shift is some kind of bitch—I mean witch. She makes us obey rules that haven't even been invented yet.

(MATRON ONE crosses to play dissonant chord on violin [the "bell" sound]. PRISONERS line up for a count. MATRON TWO transforms back to CYNTHIA.)

JOCKEY: Three.

CYNTHIA: Eleven.

CHAMP: Fifteen.

OX TAIL: Twenty-two.

EL TORO: Twenty-nine.

KATHLEEN: *(From net)* Thirty-six.

(OX TAIL transforms into HEAD MATRON. Other prisoners are still in line.)

MATRON ONE: They're bringing in a new load of prisoners.

(MATRON ONE crosses to cell, unlocks door [at O M T, rattles chain]. HEAD MATRON crosses to net, grabs KATHLEEN, who transforms into a new prisoner and is walked across the playing area and thrown in cell. The prisoners get very excited as they watch the new ones come in.)

EL TORO: Fresh fish!

JOCKEY: Hot zucchini!

(They continue to cat-call and comment on the women: they might have known "that one" from high school or "that one" from a recent local T V show. This banter continues until KATHLEEN and MATRON pass—then each woman in count line transforms into a new prisoner as KATHLEEN and MATRON pass her. Some of the women may show signs of fatigue and pain from various forms of drug addiction. Others may be jumpy and irritable from heavy drinking. Some may still bear bruises and other marks of their "apprehension" [i.e., forcible arrest]. Certain "political prisoners" may be recovering from severe burns on arms, legs, heads or faces [i.e., from being burned out of hideouts by police] or gunshot wounds. Some may be "spaced out" from past heavy drug usage; others may be cool and keep to themselves, or some are easygoing, but show no "heavy" emotion. MATRON ONE transforms into a new arrival

and joins the others who are moved en masse by the HEAD
MATRON *across the playing area toward the net. The image
the actors project during this move is one of animals being
led to slaughter, done in silence, very slowly.)*

HEAD MATRON: All right ladies, right this way.

*(Takes a prisoner by the arm and leads her to a place behind
the net)*

HEAD MATRON: Nice to see you so bright this early.

(Sends another prisoner to the net)

HEAD MATRON: Step up to the counter and verify the
list of your belongings.

(Leads another prisoner)

HEAD MATRON: This is the last time you'll see them till
you get out.

(Takes another prisoner out of line)

HEAD MATRON: If it isn't on the list now, it won't be
there when you go home.

(Sends last prisoner to the net)

*(All the new prisoners are now lined up behind the net. They
are captive there.)*

EL TORO: *(Intimately, without moving)* I feel like I've
known you all my life.

JOCKEY: Me, too.

EL TORO: Who are you?

JOCKEY: A messenger.

EL TORO: What for?

JOCKEY: To make you happy. *(Leans to kiss her)*

*(In the following section two speakers at a time say the
same lines, but with their own rhythms and intentions. In
this way, it becomes a jam.* KATHLEEN *speaks to* EL TORO
across the space between the cells and the net. CHAMP *and*

CYNTHIA *speak intimately to each other without moving—they are behind the net.)*

CHAMP & KATHLEEN: I need something.

CYNTHIA & EL TORO: I know what you need.

CHAMP & KATHLEEN: How do you know it?

CYNTHIA & EL TORO: Been watching you.

CHAMP & KATHLEEN: I been watching you, too.

CYNTHIA & EL TORO: I want to lay my head down on your breast.

CHAMP & KATHLEEN: C'mere.

(During the following confrontation, the other prisoners behind the net quietly begin to " look for a way out." All prisoners [including KATHLEEN *in the cell] participate except* RONNIE. *This continues throughout the scene. The* MATRON *maintains her distance, speaks from in front of cells toward* RONNIE, *who stands at the side of the net.)*

MATRON: What have you got in your hand?

RONNIE: Nothin'.

MATRON: I saw something flash!

RONNIE: Far out. *(Looks around)* Where?

MATRON: Don't be smart. Act like a lady.

RONNIE: If I did you'd arrest me all over again. Ladies are prostitutes, and I never hooked in my...

MATRON: Ladies are ladies, and ladies get respect.

RONNIE: Not where I come from.

MATRON: Hold out your hand or be ready to go before the disciplinary committee.

RONNIE: *(Reluctantly holds out her hand)* Yes, ma'am.

MATRON: A salt shaker?

RONNIE: Hey, you guessed it.

MATRON: That's enough.

(RONNIE *drops imaginary shaker*)

MATRON: Why'd you take it?

RONNIE: T' brighten up m' room.

MATRON: A salt shaker?

RONNIE: Different strokes for different folks.

MATRON: I'll have to report this.

RONNIE: (*Pleading now, her kidding attitude gone*) Aww, please, Mrs Frank, give me a break? I hardly knew I walked out of the dining room with it—it's just it was shiny, and it's so drab here.

MATRON: Smarten up! (*Mimes writing something in a little book*) All right, ladies, you will now line up and strip to your shoes and socks.

(*The prisoners come out from behind the net, stand in a straight line in front of it. As they do,* JOCKEY *unrolls a sheet of white paper that is attached to two poles and stretches it to the other end of the platform attaching other pole to metal holders on side of platform, thus making a scrim that covers the women from neck to mid-thigh. A light behind the net is turned on and other lights dimmed so the stripping can be seen in silhouette. The women strip to socks and shoes.*)

MATRON: Hand all your clothes to the inmate who's checked your belongings list and your clothing will be added to it. Your new ensemble will be provided by the State.

(*Articles of clothing [at O M T the green surgical robes] are passed down the line toward* JOCKEY, *at far end of line. New clothing [men's hats and sports jackets] are passed up the line. The prisoners mime dressing. They put on sport coats as they would dresses—wiggle into them, zip...they hold hats.*)

MATRON: Roll your underwear and other garments up and hand them to the personnel you see here. Speed it up. We have to get on to your space assignments.

(EL TORO *stands motionless, looking at dress [really a sports jacket but it's behind white paper]. The* HEAD MATRON *addresses her.*)

MATRON: What's the matter? Get dressed.

EL TORO: I never wore no dress before.

(HEAD MATRON *crosses to lineup, looks under the white paper, crosses away and takes line.*)

MATRON: You're a female, I see. That means you'll wear a dress here.

EL TORO: I don't think I can, Ma'am.

MATRON: You'll address me as Lieutenant Meeker.

EL TORO: I can't wear no dress, Lieutenant Meeker.

MATRON: You asking for the hole?

EL TORO: I'm sorry, Lieutenant Meeker, but it will make me sick to wear a dress.

MATRON: You have ten seconds to get it on. (*Looks at watch*) One, two, three, four, five...

(EL TORO *awkwardly pulls dress [sport coat] on and stands there, mortified.*)

MATRON: There now, you look real cute in that. Nobody dies from wearing dresses...

(EL TORO *faints in place. The other prisoners catch her, try to revive her.*)

MATRON: On your feet. You're holding up the parade.

(*Other prisoners pull* EL TORO *up*)

MATRON: (*Quieting them down, regaining control*) All right, ladies, you will now pledge allegiance.

(*All jump to attention, put their hands to hearts*)

MATRON: We will sing our new, special "Fight
Depression" song, so thoughtfully written by our own
Miss Schnauzer's grandfather.

*(The women burst through the paper screen, wearing men's
hats and sports jackets over their dresses. HEAD MATRON
transforms back into OX TAIL. She wears sports jacket under
guard coat which she removes and joins the others. The
subtext of this song is the prisoners' fantasy of themselves as
pop-art criminals.)*

PRISONERS: *(Sing)*
Tighten your belt and
Tough it out.
Some lamebrains born
On the prairies,
Or in the smog-soaked
Basins;
Starved into
Staring awareness,
And suspicious
Short-order cooks
By the Depression—the
"Great Depression" that is—
Have stuffed their faith
Up in holy argyle socks and
Play a loner's game;
Sneaking
On slippery dewy limbs
Fall into spider nets
Saying "I know exactly where I am
At all times. I planned it. I planned it."
I'm the best damn Sunday morning quarterback
Who ever lived
And if you doubt it, I'll
Start phoning you long distance
At three o'clock in the morning.
My goal-posts are always up

And painted day-glow white.
That's right!
I never sleep
Because I keep
An open eye
On history.
Thirty thousand years from now
I want to see it written—"He sold Orange
Julius to the Chinese,
Quadraphonic to the Sudanese,
A (Insert two-syllable name of local fast food store—
i. e., McDonald's or Dairy Queen) on every
Kremlin corner.
Arabs drive Continentals,
While Saddam sleeps
Steely eyed wide
On a Sealy Posturepedic.
Chilean-Brazilian generals reside in
Amphibious Cadillacs,
Hubcaps engraved
With images of doves who
Carry Picasso's eyes
Blazing in their talons."

(The women peel off their sports coats. The next three lines are said simultaneously as KATHLEEN *goes back to her cell,* RONNIE *and the other prisoners go back behind the net.* EL TORO *remains in the central playing area.)*

EL TORO: The first time I tried to kill myself…

RONNIE: I tried to kill myself lots of times.

KATHLEEN: I tried to kill myself three times.

EL TORO: *(Alone in the center space addresses audience)* …I waited till everyone was gone to work… *(Stops suddenly, looks around, relives fantasy of what it was like to be out on the streets. She feels she is being followed by something. When she is sure she is no longer followed, she continues. This continues throughout the scene in places indicated*) ...then I got this Japanese carbine that my Dad brought back from the South Pacific... (*Stops, looks around, waits, goes on*) ...and I went into the hall closet with it. (*Takes a breath, looks around, continues*) First I tried to put the barrel of the gun to my temple, but the closet was too small for that. (*Stops, looks, waits, goes on*) So then I remember reading a story in the *Enquirer* about how this guy had blown his head off by putting this shotgun in his mouth— (*Inhales deeply as she says*)-so-o-o-o-o-o-o-o-o-, (*Shapes her hand like a pistol, sticks the barrel in her mouth, rotates in a circle with this image so the audience can see, curls up in a ball on the floor*) And I pulled the trigger.

RONNIE: (*From the net*) But I never had enough pills to keep me out more than twenty-four hours. Except for the time they kept me in the hole for three months—I lost my mind.

(JOCKEY *transforms into* MATRON THREE, *puts on guard coat, pushes cart center; crosses to pull* RONNIE *from behind net and places her in cart,* EL TORO *continues speaking and moving all around center area. The cart is solitary confinement, a cell on wheels that is moved up and down the center space by* MATRON THREE. RONNIE *tries desperately to get out. She scratches messages on the floor with her fingernails, bangs her head against the bars.*)

EL TORO: (*From floor*) It tasted of oil, and lint... (*Rises*) ...and shit. (*Stops abruptly, looks around, listens, relaxes, goes on*) ...Then I realized I needed a shell for the gun, but it was a Jap gun, and none of the shells around the house would fit it. I got so mad I threw the gun down, and I decided I'd have to move out since I couldn't find nothing to use to kill myself. From that day on I was a lot happier—all I had to do was move out. Why did it take me so long to find that out?

(MATRON THREE *crosses to* KATHLEEN *in cell—she is being prepared for a medical examination.*)

EL TORO: If it's rotten you move—simple as that. Pack up and move out. *(Joins others behind the net)*

MATRON THREE: *(To* KATHLEEN*)* Give me your bra.

KATHLEEN: Watch out, it'll burn ya.

MATRON THREE: No talking. One more wisecrack and you go to the hole.

(KATHLEEN *opens her mouth, then closes it.*)

MATRON THREE: Shoes, cigarettes, wristwatch, rings.

(Reaching out from cell to MATRON *like a balancing act,* KATHLEEN *offers some part of her body—leg, heart, neck— as each item is called for.*)

MATRON THREE: Get up on the table and prepare for your enema.

(KATHLEEN *looks at her, sneers and shrugs.*)

RONNIE: *(From solitary where she's been pounding on floor to find a loose board. She rattles bars—the* MATRONS *who guard her are expressionless and unhearing. They or* MATRON THREE *turn the cart in a circular fashion in the center area.)* Let me out of here! You evil bastard bitches—your hair is on fire, and snakes with blazing fangs live between yer yellow teeth—I seen 'em, I seen 'em. Let me out of here. You hear me! You stinkin' shitheads, ya motherfuckin' dirty daughters of the Jesus lickers—I tell you once and for all, let me out of here! I'll kick this place in and tear you limb from limb, *(Climbs to highest point of cart rail)* and use yer ribs to spear yer hearts, you farts! *(Standing free on top rail)* You can't keep me in here—I won't stay in here!—Don't you know who I am? You let me out of here right now, you sinning, grinning, stuffed-assed satans. *(Jumps down)* Let me out! Right now! I command you! Let me out! *(Continues "Let me out!" as a demand, a plea, beating herself up, etc.)* Let me out! Let me out of here! *(Looks for a way out)*

(RONNIE's chanting of "Let me out!" incites supportive outcries from the other women behind the net. This becomes a jam of different intentions for the "Let me out!" outcry. It continues through the next three speeches.)

KATHLEEN: *(From the cells—comes right in overlapping "Let me out...!")* I really didn't know who I was—I just knew I couldn't take the pain any more. I felt like the sharpest axe was wedged right down my head between my eyes and sinking lower every minute— every single minute the axe was cutting me. It would get to the bottom of my brain, and then another axe would start at the top of my head and slice right down beside the first axe. Not in the same place, but like slicing salami, neat and in a row. The pain of the slicing kept right on. Let me out!

RONNIE: Let me out!

ALL PRISONERS: Let me out!

CYNTHIA: *(Jumps out from behind net to immediately in front of it)* I didn't have no clothes—only a blood-soaked, pissed-out mattress, and a hole in the floor— and it was so cold, the cold ate at my hands and toes as sharp as the axe in my head.

(Lunges and throws herself on cart—MATRON shakes her loose.)

CYNTHIA: I turned into an animal, but smart. *(Mimes picking up spoon from floor, threatens audience.)* I kept a spoon. I told them it had fallen down the shit hole, and I sharpened that spoon—I made that spoon so sharp I could cut my hair with it. Then when it got sharp enough, I lay down on the cold cement floor and I cut both my wrists. Let me out! *(Lies flat on floor)*

RONNIE: Let me out!

KATHLEEN: Let me out!

CHAMP: *(Comes out from behind net to floor)* I can't tell you what a great feeling that was—the pain started to run out of my head, *(Lowers herself onto* CYNTHIA's *body)* right onto the floor. And I was beginning to relax at last, feeling the pressure just sigh right on out of me. *(Sits up—jam of "Let me out!" stops.)* I'd been waiting and waiting and waiting for that feeling. See— *(Shows the audience a real scar)*—here's the scar. See there?

(Each woman shows one member of the audience a scar she has on her wrist, arm, face, neck, etc. saying:)

EACH PRISONER: See? See there?

(All women enter the solitary cell [the cart]. They mime being chained to it by their wrists and pivot in a circle in the center area [at O M T JOCKEY *pushed with one foot while* OX TAIL *walked it around—she is tethered to the rail of the cart like ox in a yoke]. They testify to the pain of their situation with their hands.)*

RONNIE: *(In midst of the others)* But they put me in the hospital and sewed me up. I was so mad they brought me back, I tried to throw things at the nurses. I pulled the tubes out of my arms, but they just kept putting them back. It was so beautiful to die, just like I thought it would be. It was so warm, and my grandmother was waiting for me with her arms out like this—and just as I was going to run into her arms they brought me back. After I healed up they put me back in the hole. I had to eat with my fingers—they wouldn't give me no spoons.

*(*RONNIE *joins others in testifying with their hands tied to the rail of the cart. The prisoners sing in harmony.)*

PRISONERS: Jesus walked
This lonesome valley.

He had to walk
It by himself.
Oh, nobody else
Could walk it for him.
He had to walk it by himself.
We must walk
This lonesome valley.
We have to walk
It by ourselves.
Oh, nobody else
Can walk it for us.
We have to walk it by ourselves.

(They break out of the cart, move to positions across playing area, and taking a vigorous, positive attitude, sing the song as a joyous gospel.)

PRISONERS: You "gotta go"
And stand your trial.
You "gotta go"
And stand it by yourself.
Oh, nobody else
Can stand it for you.
You gotta go and stand it by yourself
Yourself!

(EL TORO drops to her knees and begins to scrub toward center of the playing area. From the opposite end of the playing area, CYNTHIA scrubs toward her, closer and closer to her. She stares at EL TORO, smiles, tries to catch her eye, clears her throat or lets her brush get away from her so that they somehow touch or get very close.)

CYNTHIA: *(Very quietly)* I know who you are.

(EL TORO freezes.)

CYNTHIA: Don't worry. Lotsa people love you.

(EL TORO slowly but deliberately scrubs away from her.)

CYNTHIA: Really, don't worry. I'm not gonna blow yer cover.

(In a rage, JOCKEY *charges across the floor.)*

JOCKEY: *(Points roughly at* CYNTHIA*)* I'm gonna get you—

(To two other prisoners walking across the space)

JOCKEY: —and then I'm gonna get *you*—and then *(To* EL TORO*)* I'm gonna get you.

CYNTHIA: *(Stands between* JOCKEY *and* EL TORO*)* Oh no yer not, because first ya gotta go through me.

*(*JOCKEY *shoves* CYNTHIA *away, grabs* EL TORO *by the collar and starts to knock her around—*EL TORO *starts to laugh.)*

EL TORO: Keep it up and one day you might connect.

JOCKEY: *(Frustrated)* You told Betsie you were going to take Dana away from me.

EL TORO: Nobody can take anyone unless they're ready to go.

JOCKEY: *(Lunges at* EL TORO*)* You bitch!

EL TORO: *(Freeing herself)* Butch—that's *butch.*

CYNTHIA: *(Cracking up)* Ya don't wanna get all messed…

JOCKEY: I'm gonna fix yer mouth so's you won't be able to ever eat again, let alone kiss anyone. *(Lunges at* EL TORO*)*

EL TORO: *(Playing with* JOCKEY*)* Keep holding my collar just like that.

(They dance together.)

EL TORO: Yes, that's it, a perfect tilt to the chin and a one and a two and a…

(EL TORO *lets* JOCKEY *have it. On the way down,* JOCKEY *snatches* EL TORO'S *glasses and smashes them.*)

JOCKEY: *(Threatening)* I'll put out yer eyes, you creep, you twerp. You can't move in on me.

EL TORO: *(Standing ground)* Give me back my glasses, you motherfucker, or I'll sit on your rotten guts till they burst that yellow shit out all over our nice clean floor.

CYNTHIA: *(Taking* EL TORO *by the hand)* Let's get the fuck outa here.

EL TORO: *(Resisting)* I want her head—I'm gonna blast it open. She's got my glasses.

(JOCKEY, EL TORO *and* CYNTHIA *run out.*)

RONNIE: *(She's been keeping watch from cell)* Run. We'll get it. Come on.

(*In the cells* KATHLEEN, RONNIE *[whose "code" name is* GARY*],* CHAMP *and* JOCKEY *are talking.* KATHLEEN *and* RONNIE *are in one cell,* CHAMP *and* JOCKEY *in another. The rest of the women transform into other prisoners. The transformation is seen through changes in their walks as they move through the yard, to the warden's office, or back to their cells. With each new walk, the prisoners give themselves a new destination.*)

KATHLEEN: What's wrong?

GARY: Nothin'.

KATHLEEN: *(Hugging her)* What you mean, nothin'? Tears streaming down your face all morning.

CHAMP: She's always blue about something.

GARY: *(Shaking* KATHLEEN *off)* It's my anniversary.

CHAMP: Why, you should be happy.

KATHLEEN: Yeah—I don't have anniversaries. I wish I had an anniversary. I done broke up with everyone!

GARY: Not mine you wouldn't.

JOCKEY: *(To* CHAMP*)* It's the anniversary of her coming out of the closet.

CHAMP: Yeah, you can still see the splinters in her fists, where she was pounding on the door.

*(*CHAMP *and* JOCKEY *hit each other and laugh and laugh.)*

GARY: You two are so tough, you miss out on really feeling anything.

KATHLEEN: *(Approaching gently)* Aw, don't mind them—they just like to show off. *(Embracing her)* Are you in love, honey.

GARY: Oh yes. I love a strong man. He stood up to the whole world. He taught me how to take it. I can do easy time because of him. I know I'm going to see him again. Today's our anniversary. Two weeks ago the pigs shot him.

KATHLEEN: *(Holding* GARY*)* Oh honey, I'm so sorry.

CHAMP: *(To* KATHLEEN*)* You gonna fall for that?

JOCKEY: *(To* CHAMP*)* Kick it off—don't hurt her more. You're as bad as the pigs.

CHAMP: *(Pulling up her fist and threatening* JOCKEY*)* Take that back.

JOCKEY: Simmer down.

*(*CHAMP *and* JOCKEY *wrestle in cell.)*

GARY: *(At* CHAMP *and* JOCKEY*)* You are as bad as the pigs. Fight and shoot, shoot and fight.

CHAMP: *(Pinning* JOCKEY *to the floor)* You're lying.

GARY: It's my anniversary.

CHAMP: Anniversary of your biggest lie.

GARY: I'm not lying.

CHAMP: *(Gets up, moves to bars)* Yea, you are. When I got here you told me your name was Tania.

GARY: Shut up.

CHAMP: You name isn't Tania, is it?

GARY: That was one of my names. But you're not to say it out loud.

CHAMP: You want to know her new code name? It's Gary. Who ever heard of a femme calling herself Gary Gilmore.

*(*KATHLEEN, *who has continued to try to comfort* GARY, *backs off.)*

GARY: *(No longer looking at* CHAMP*)* I'm calling you crazy. No one would do that.

CHAMP: *(To others)* She told me in the shower her new name was Gary.

GARY: They shot him. He wanted me to go with him.

CHAMP: Tell the others you made it up.

GARY: You're too coarse to understand. It's between his spirit and mine.

CHAMP: There ain't nothin' between you and him but six feet of dirt.

GARY: He lives through me.

CHAMP: He was shot at sunrise.

GARY: I took his name to keep him alive.

CHAMP: *(Swings out of her cell, struts across yard)* Don't you wish you'd met him, baby. You never met a bad-ass like that. The most you ever had was a toothless Hell's Angel who stole you away from your Granddaddy's trailer camp. *(Turns to* RONNIE /GARY *and mocks her.)* He shoved his tongue in your ear when he stole you away and you fell madly in love with his gun and his bike—ain't that right?

(RONNIE/GARY *jumps from her cell and goes after* CHAMP.)

GARY: You bitch!

CHAMP: *(Trying to hold her off)* See what I mean. Holier Than Thou! Look at this wildcat.

GARY: I'm him and he's me, now.

CHAMP: Next thing you'll be Hanoi Hannah and Tokyo Rose.

GARY: They pardoned her, you dope.

CHAMP: You're the dope, you doped-out nut.

GARY: *(Pulling self away)* You're so square you don't know nothing—you're only Champ. I can be as many people as I want to be.

CHAMP: *(To audience and other prisoners)* See what I mean. She makes her life up out of the T V news.

GARY: *(Lunges at her)* You make your life up out of comic books.

CHAMP: There's a difference?

(They fight fiercely, rolling around on the floor, scratching and kicking. The other prisoners stop and watch, cheer for one or the other, or keep walking so as not to get involved.)

GARY: *(During the fight)* I'm in love. I'm in love with the whole world.

(They continue to fight ferociously. The WARDEN's *voice comes over the loudspeaker.)*

WARDEN: Ladies!

*(*CHAMP *and* RONNIE *and all prisoners freeze, look toward voice and listen.)*

WARDEN: Ladies!

*(*RONNIE *and* CHAMP *separate as if nothing had been going on.)*

WARDEN: Please proceed to your cells.

(PRISONERS *run to the cells from wherever they are. They move from cell to cell, cleaning, stashing contraband. Twinkle lights flash as the* WARDEN *continues.)*

WARDEN: Dress appropriately for Sunday worship. Today we will be graced by a visit from the Pentecostal Church. Cells must be cleaned and left in pristine condition as if the Legislature were visiting us. Remember, you are Christian Ladies who keep your houses Christian clean. Your room and your person are reflections of what is going on inside. If you have a messy room or present a messy person, what can anyone think but that your head is a mess...

(PRISONERS *run to area in front of net, Put on "Ladies" hats and transform into members of the Pentecostal Church)*

WARDEN: ...and therefore, a perfect workshop for the Devil? Ladies, give thought to cleanliness, dress in your Sunday best, and then proceed to the chapel. Give our visitors your undivided attention. They've come a long way to bring us Good News.

(The area in front of net is suddenly bathed in bright light. The piano, accordion or violin begins to play church chords. The Pentecostal Church Members are huddled together, terrified of the prisoners. RONNIE *has transformed into the* HEAD WOMAN *who gives the others strength and sends them into the jail to spread the good word as she speaks.)*

HEAD WOMAN: *(Church chords continue under her speech.)* You are in the funhouse...

(She holds OX TAIL, *one of the parishioners, who goes bravely into the prison)*

HEAD WOMAN: ...of the Lord.

(Touches two more women, EL TORO *and* CYNTHIA, *who receive strength and go forth bravely)*

HEAD WOMAN: But be very careful...

(Gives strength to another woman, JOCKEY, *who moves onto the floor)*

HEAD WOMAN: …that you do not make fun of the Holy Ghost.

(Holds CHAMP *and sends her off)*

(The Pentecostals are gathered together in the center playing area. They are less terrified after being reassured by the HEAD WOMAN, *but they still hold onto one another while reaching out to the prisoners [at O M T the audience became the prisoners in the actors' minds at this point] to spread the faith for their salvation.)*

ALL PARISHONERS: *(Sing)*
Even if you don't know how to pray
The ghost within you does.
Listen
Listen
Listen
Listen.
Let the maimed ape have her say.
Let your English mind
Get lost, go blind—;
Take the plunge and speak in tongues.
Mother song
And father sound,
Take the plunge
And speak in tongues.
Listen
Listen
Listen.

(During the second verse of Speak in Tongues, CYNTHIA *and* RONNIE *as parishoners come together center. They are excited.* OX TAIL *and* EL TORO *continue to sing and preach—they have clearly taken the role of Pentecostal ministers. The ministers sense the new excitement—they*

direct their energies to CYNTHIA *and* RONNIE, *who separate and begin to look inward.)*

CHAMP, EL TORO, JOCKEY & KATHLEEN: *(Sing as parishoners)*
Even if you don't know how to pray
The ghost within you does.

OX TAIL: *(As minister directs energy toward* RONNIE*)*
Listen
Listen
Listen
*(*OX TAIL *touches* RONNIE.*)*
Let the maimed ape have...

*(*RONNIE *screams, possessed, falls to floor and is caught by* JOCKEY. *She begins to speak in tongues. She raises, still speaking in tongues and moves in a rhythmic dance.)*

OX TAIL: ...her say.

EL TORO: *(As ministerdirects energy toward* CYNTHIA*)*
Take the plunge...

*(*CYNTHIA *screams, possessed, falls and is caught by* KATHLEEN. *She begins to speak in tongues, rises and moves in a rhythmic dance.)*

EL TORO: ...and speak in tongues.
Mother song
And father sound.

(As the song Speak in Tongues *comes to an end, other members of the group become obsessed, fall to the floor and speak in tongues. As the speaking goes on, they let their tongues direct the movement of their bodies until they are lifted off the floor and go into rhythmic dance. Parishoners who speak in tongues during the song keep the volume down, allowing it to rise when the singers are silent.* KATHLEEN *and* JOCKEY *[still as parishoners] scream, possessed. Then they begin to speak in tongues and rhythmically move in dance. With parishoners speaking in tongues,* OX TAIL *as*

MINISTER ONE *and* EL TORO *as* MINISTER TWO *come to the center and pray.)*

MINISTER ONE: I pray to the Lord with all my heart and soul to give me the grace and understanding to interpret the message you are sending here. Especially for all the souls gathered here today in your name. Hallelujah, praise the Lord. The Power is moving. The Power is speaking.

(She is drawn to CYNTHIA, *who is speaking in tongues, and lays her hands on her.)*

MINISTER ONE: Praise the Lord. Hallelujah. This sweet soul saying…

*(*CYNTHIA *becomes silent as her speaking in tongues is translated by the minister.)*

MINISTER ONE: "Bask in the light and believe, sister and believe, brothers. The Lord is here—we are blessed and loved if we will only open up our hearts." Do you believe? I believe! Praise the Lord!

*(*CYNTHIA *continues to move rhythmically in celebration. She no longer speaks in tongues.)*

MINISTER TWO: Praise the Lord!

(Moves to RONNIE *who is speaking in tongues, lays hands on her)*

MINISTER TWO: And this dear child of God, this believer is saying to us brothers and sisters… What?

(Pulls Tongues *speech from* RONNIE *and translates—* RONNIE *is silenced.)*

MINISTER TWO: …"This container is too small…" *(Puzzles over this for a moment, then bows head, smiles and looks up)* Thank you, Lord.

RONNIE: *(Dancing rhythmically in celebration)* Thank you, Jesus.

MINISTER ONE: Praise the Lord, Hallelujah! God is sending me the ability to translate this divine message into English.

MINISTER TWO: The message is coming now, through this instrument who speaks in tongues—

MINISTER ONE: —this instrument created in God's image.

(MINISTERS ONE *and* TWO *lay hands on* KATHLEEN *and* JOCKEY *who are still speaking in tongues. Looking up into the light, they begin to translate—at first haltingly, then building with full confidence.* JOCKEY *and* KATHLEEN *stop speaking as their tongues are translated.*)

MINISTER TWO: The answer to the question, "Where are the women inventors and artists of the past?" is…

(*The* MINISTERS *move to the center of the playing area, stand back to back and move in a circle. Each revelation comes to them like a bolt of lightning.*)

MINISTER ONE: They were in the kitchen inventing corn bread.

MINISTER TWO: They were in the kitchen inventing chili.

MINISTER ONE: They were in the kitchen inventing granola.

MINISTER TWO: They were in the kitchen inventing salad.

MINISTER ONE: They were in the kitchen inventing meatloaf.

MINISTER TWO: They were in the kitchen inventing egg foo young.

MINISTER ONE: They were in the kitchen inventing knishes.

MINISTER TWO: They were in the kitchen inventing the hot dog.

MINISTER ONE: They were in the kitchen inventing spaghetti.

MINISTER TWO: They were in the kitchen inventing pancakes.

MINISTER ONE: They were in the kitchen inventing butter.

MINISTER TWO: They were in the kitchen inventing fire.

MINISTER ONE: They were in the bedroom inventing quilts.

MINISTER TWO: They were in the bathroom inventing perfume.

MINISTER ONE: They were in the bathroom inventing soap.

MINISTER TWO: They were in the bathroom inventing the bath.

MINISTER ONE: They were in the sewing room inventing clothes.

MINISTER TWO: They were in the earth inventing farming.

MINISTER ONE: They were in the woods inventing dancing.

MINISTER ONE: They were by the waterfall inventing singing.

(Both MINISTERS *remove their hats.)*

MINISTER ONE: *(As* OX TAIL, *her prisoner self)* They were in your arms—inventing loving.

(All parishoners take off their hats. A very, very brief smile to audience. Then all run to the television room area in front of cells and sit down to watch T V. Throughout this scene they rearrange and knock each other around to get the best

view of the T V. KATHLEEN *is in her cell, separated from the rest, but also watches the T V.)*

CHAMP: I'm sick of Sesame Street!

EL TORO: The Warden loves it.

KATHLEEN: Change the channel.

JOCKEY: I wanna see…

RONNIE: *(Covering* JOCKEY's *mouth)* Close your mouth and maybe you can.

JOCKEY: Your mother sucks worms.

RONNIE: That's what yer Daddy's got fer a dick.

JOCKEY: I'm gonna tie you to the wall and you got to watch Sesame Street forever.

RONNIE: I'd rather watch that than your ugly mug.

CHAMP: Be cool. Be cool.

EL TORO: Mrs Johnson's gonna put you in the hole.

RONNIE: Where you was born.

JOCKEY: Right behind you. You was born out of a behind.

RONNIE: Shithead.

JOCKEY: You look like the garbage can on the T V show.

RONNIE: Lame, you're too dumb to fight with.

JOCKEY: I get my ideas from the cookie monster.

KATHLEEN: The Munsters have returned.

EL TORO: Morticia, let's start burning the bodies.

CHAMP: Here, light 'em with vampire piss—it works faster than lighter fluid.

KATHLEEN: Shut up, all of you—I'm trying to learn to spell.

RONNIE: The hell with you. *(Singing)* "Take me away baby, baby. Come closer to me and I'll give you my secret key."

CHAMP: Turn up the show and drown out that cat in heat.

(CYNTHIA and EL TORO transform into MATRON ONE and MATRON TWO. They put on coats by the cells and walk toward the Warden's area, keeping a careful eye on members of the audience, nodding at someone they know, looking for contraband, stopping any trouble they see. When they reach the net, they keep watch, then do the following as a "conductor" exercise.)

MATRON ONE: *(As they watch OX TAIL)* She's so cool all the time.

MATRON TWO: Is she real or acting?

MATRON ONE: Anyone who winds up here and acts as sweet as that has got to be acting.

MATRON TWO: She'll do easy time then.

MATRON ONE: Not if I get to her.

MATRON TWO: You're taking this job too serious.

MATRON ONE: What else is there to do? God put me on this earth for a reason. I'm a good wife. I try and pray to be a good mother, and if I can help one other person, then my life will be worthwhile.

MATRON TWO: She's so sweet. Are you sure it's an act?

MATRON ONE: The Warden said if we can get her angry and fighting, then sure as shootin' we can "get through" and help her straighten out.

MATRON TWO: But it takes so much energy to deal with them when they fight back.

MATRON ONE: You're a Christian, aren't you?

MATRON TWO: Of course I'm a Christian!

MATRON ONE: Then take pity on that poor girl, and do what you have to do to get her to see the light.

MATRON TWO: I admire you—I really, really do. I try hard to be a good Christian, but I'm not clear all the time in my mind, just what's the right way to go about...

MATRON ONE: I never have any doubt about what is right and what is wrong. I never have had—my Daddy and Mama taught me that real early.

(They take one last look at the yard, then march back to the cells, keeping their eyes on both sides of the audience as they go. MATRON TWO transforms back into EL TORO. CYNTHIA remains MATRON ONE and rattles chain on cells, signaling the women to come down into the yard for recreation. PRISONERS wear gym shorts and "Coyote" [the prostitutes' union] T-shirts. Some are doing calisthenics, some basketball, jump rope, run in place, etc. Cell lights and twinkle lights come up abruptly on RONNIE's cell.)

RONNIE: *(Very "spaced out")* I got busted last summer in Colorado Springs. What a lousy jail. All we got to eat twice a day was cold oatmeal, nothin' to put on it, and coffee made o' sewer water. They gave us Top tobacco to smoke. Stale—it was so stale, I like to set my eyebrows on fire ev'r' time I lit up. *Whoooooosh* like the Fourth O' July. Went to the hospital with second-degree burns on my eyelids. No shit. No shit! They finally felt so bad about it they let me out for only six bucks. So I high-tailed it for Boulder. There I spent three beautiful days with this spaced-out dude in a bare van. There was nothing in this big Dodge van but, get this, man—nothing in it but this giant black leather rocking chair. This spaced-out dude, he had this chair built just for him for tripping. He loved that chair so much he took it on vacation with him. Hooked this fucking chair right up to the generator, and man,

he'd sit in it, drop P C P, M B D, acid, and half my
thorazines, and he'd rock himself into ecstatic oblivion.
You know what he had built into the seat of his chair?
—vibrator, man. *(Pause)* Far out!

(Lights come down on RONNIE, *up on* EL TORO, *who stands
behind the net—she is high on pills.)*

EL TORO: Hi, my name's Toro. Man, I'm clean, no
shit. Wanna see my arms? Look. *(Rolls up sleeves)* See
there—you can't see no tracks there. I quit the needle.
I quit it. I quit the needle and I cut my hair. See how
clean and neat I look, just like they want me. Never
found my real mother till I was sixteen. Ain't that right,
Champ?

CHAMP: *(Doing calisthenics in the yard)* That's right,
Toro.

EL TORO: This here is my friend Champ. We was
together in reform school. We was there four or five
years. Hell, Champ was born there—right, Champ? We
been in forever. We know the score—right, Champ?

CHAMP: Right.

EL TORO: *(Rolls up sleeves again)* See them arms? When
I first kissed my husband I fell right in love with him.
Just like that, my knees went just like this. *(Wiggles
knees, "makes like" to faint)* I went home and told my
Mom—I hadn't known my Mom too long at the time—
it took me so fuckin' long to find her—but I told her,
I'm gonna marry that guy, and sure enough, four
weeks later we was married, and four weeks after that
I started on the needle. But then he ratted on me, so I
shot him. You seen the bullet holes, didn't you Champ?

CHAMP: I seen 'em, Toro.

(After her speech, RONNIE *comes down from her cell, puts
on a guard coat and transforms into a* MATRON. *She doesn't
hear* EL TORO, *who's in another part of the building. She*

signals to other prisoners that recreation is over and they must scrub the floor. She throws scrub brushes to them.)

EL TORO: Sure enough. But we got lucky and we're still in love. Then we got busted together for dealing—he's in prison at the men's penal complex.

CHAMP: The penis complex.

EL TORO: Right, that's what I got. Anyway, we got lucky and we're still in love, he didn't die, but what a rat he was. Well, I can't help it—I did fall in love with him, just like lightning striking…that's the way it was.

(Lights come down on EL TORO. Focus shifts to the floor where the prisoners are scrubbing, covering sections of the floor in pairs: OX TAIL and CHAMP, CYNTHIA and EL TORO [who has come down and joined her], JOCKEY and KATHLEEN.)

MATRON: *(Talks down to prisoners)* You ladies should be down like that on your knees three times a day, thanking the good Lord you were born in this time, in this country.

(MATRON's attention shifts, with crowlike eyes, to the audience—eyes darting from one person to another each time the prisoners sing. PRISONERS sing to each other, then tenderly caress, cuddle and make love to each other, always keeping an eye on the matron to be sure that her eyes are elsewhere. When the MATRON speaks, the women begin furiously scrubbing.)

OX TAIL: *(Sings to CHAMP)*
You may put your head down,
You may sink into the pillows of love.

JOCKEY: *(Sings to KATHLEEN)*
You may put your hand down,
You may unclench your fist,
You may unlock your joints.

(PRISONERS *separate and go back to fierce scrubbing when they hear the* MATRON *say:*)

MATRON: Before this great country was made into a country, you, Jockey, you, Ox Tail, and you, Champ, would 'a been hanged. Just like that. No ifs ands or buts. Taken out and hanged by your neck until you were dead...for stealing, for picking pockets. No pleading, no mercy—out! Hanged!

(MATRON *changes focus to the audience, looking for contraband, sudden movements, anything suspicious.* PRISONERS *sing and tenderly caress one another,* MATRON *still oblivious.*)

CYNTHIA: *(Sings to* EL TORO*)*
You may put your head down,
You my sink into the pillows of love.

KATHLEEN: *(Sings to* JOCKEY*)*
EL TORO: *(Sings to* CYNTHIA*)*
CHAMP: *(Sings to* OX TAIL*)*
You may put your belly down.
The Lord will provide.
There is no need to strive
For food or drink.

(PRISONERS *separate and scrub:*)

MATRON: For a misdemeanor they'd cut off your hands. For adultery, a brand on your forehead—a big brand right here in the middle of your forehead—and without a valium yet.

(PRISONERS *join hands, dance in a circle around the* MATRON, *who doesn't see them because she's watching the audience.*)

PRISONERS: *(Sing)* Music will fill
All the empty spaces.
You may lay away need,
Dissolve desire.

(They spin out, reform with same partners, go to three separate areas of the floor.)

CYNTHIA, JOCKEY & OX TAIL: *(Sing)* Stay a while.

CHAMP, EL TORO & KATHLEEN: *(Sing)* Stay a while.

JOCKEY & KATHLEEN: *(Sing in center section)*
Hello eye—may I have the next dance?
Hello lips—be still now.

(PRISONERS *scrub.*)

MATRON: You don't know how lucky you are, ladies. How'd you like that, El Toro—get those pretty hands of yours cut off, for bad checks—both of them? How'd you like that?

JOCKEY: I'd like it, because then I'd be done with you!

(MATRON turns quickly, signals her to get back to work)

EL TORO: *(Sings)* Your heart beats out our trance.

CHAMP: *(Sings)* Hello tongue—this trip has just begun.

ALL PRISONERS & MATRON: *(Sing)* This is the place
Where light is feed.
The Lord will provide.
I've got what you need.
You may hide your sweet,
Burdened head
In this dancing bed.

(The prisoners continue scrubbing. EL TORO quickly and cautiously scrubs toward JOCKEY, stares at her, smiles, tries to catch her eye, clears her throat, or lets her brush get away from her so that they somehow touch or get very close.)

EL TORO: *(Very quietly)* I know who you are.

(JOCKEY *freezes*)

EL TORO: Don't worry. Lotsa people love you…

(JOCKEY *deliberately scrubs away from* EL TORO.)

EL TORO: Really, don't worry. I'm not gonna blow yer cover.

(EL TORO *and* JOCKEY *freeze. Lights come down slowly.*)

END OF ACT ONE

ACT TWO

(More new women prisoners are being admitted. They enter in darkness and take their places behind the net. As the lights come up, they project images of " looking for a way out". The group stops and listens, moves together, stops together. They range in age from seventeen to sixty. Those who've never been to prison before might keep their eyes downcast [they try to minimize their presence]. The political prisoners hold themselves erect and proud. They size up the situation and try to make contact with those with whom they can establish "lines" of sympathy. "Repeaters" are greeted like alums returning to an old school, by both inmates and guards with hearty recognition. CHAMP *is not among the prisoners—she enters the yard as* MATRON.*)*

MATRON: Take a chair, ladies. When your name is called, come forward to claim your property and valuables—and, I repeat—check the list. Bessie Mayo.

KATHLEEN: *(Transformed into* BETSY*)* That's Betsy!

MATRON: The name on the official Department list is Bessie, so that's your name.

BETSY: They wrote it down wrong.

MATRON: *(Flat tone, calling out again)* Bessie Mayo.

BETSY: My name is Betsy. I won't be called a name not my own.

MATRON: You are in prison. You have no more rights. You gave up your rights when you committed the crime that sent you here. The name on my list, written here by the Authorities, is Bessie Mayo.

BETSY: Betsy!

MATRON: Any more outbursts and you'll be taken to Adjustment.

EL TORO: Shut up, honey, and do like she says, or they throw you in the hole.

BETSY: I protest this deliberate dehumanizing process. You are beginning by taking away my own name. Well, it's going to stop right here, because I will not tolerate...

MATRON: Oh, swell, we got a Commie in this bunch. Take her away.

(BETSY *backs away from the net. The following roll call may be added to or changed at any given performance to include some names of audience members or newsworthy people. The actors transform to these different personalities. We used a set order in which the actors always responded: [1]* EL TORO *[2]* JOCKEY *[3]* RONNIE, *etc.*)

MATRON: Adelle Novas.

ADELLE: Here.

MATRON: Marijane Scoppetone.

MARIJANE: Here.

MATRON: Maimie Eisenhower.

MAIMIE: Here.

MATRON: Ida Lupino.

IDA: Here.

MATRON: Happy Ford.

HAPPY: Here.

(PRISONERS *begin to come out from behind the net and line up in front of it.*)

MATRON: Betty Rockefeller.

BETTY: Here.

MATRON: Louise Lasser.

LOUISE: Here.

MATRON: Tricia DietRite.

TRICIA: Here.

MATRON: Amy Carter.

AMY: Here.

MATRON: Marlena Dexadrine.

MARLENE: Here.

(MATRON *crosses to net, turns, removes her jacket and becomes a prisoner. She joins the others, who are acting out their fantasies of what they'll do and be when they get out. They dream of being safe-crackers, tennis champs, typists, etc.*)

JOCKEY: (*Sings, as others continue acting out their fantasies*)
When I get out of here
I'm gonna make so much money
I'll never have any fear. (*Runs onto floor and sits*)

RONNIE: (*Sings*) When I get out of here...

(*Punches others, who fall like dominoes*)

RONNIE: I'm gonna dress so sharp (*Jives on floor*) And keep my eyes piercing clear.

(CYNTHIA *and* OX TAIL *pick up* JOCKEY, EL TORO *picks up* RONNIE, *both groups perform flying images.* CHAMP *and* KATHLEEN *perform images singly.*)

RONNIE: I'll buy me a Lear jet
And you can bet—

ALL: I'm gonna fly, I'm gonna fly.

RONNIE: I'm gonna go go go go go go go go go go!
(Flying image ends.)

KATHLEEN: *(Sings, with others keeping time from floor)*
When I get out of here
I'll get me so much bread
They'll think I invented dough

ALL: *(Sing)* I'll jet by so high you won't see me go,
I'll jet by so high you won't see me go,
I'll jet by so high you won't see me go!
I'll be so high,
I'll be so high,
You won't see me go go go go go go go go go go!

(JOCKEY, OX TAIL and KATHLEEN transform into MATRON ONE, MATRON TWO and MATRON THREE. MATRON ONE begins to harass a prisoner and push her around for no visible reason. [She may not have scrubbed floor properly, or she may have been seen "with" another prisoner.] MATRONS TWO and THREE intervene, causing MATRON ONE to let prisoners go, then they bring MATRON ONE with them to the WARDEN's area where all three keep watch on the yard.)

MATRON ONE: I did what I had to do.

MATRON TWO: You kept control.

MATRON THREE: Best of all, you kept control of *yourself.*

MATRON ONE: I'm a human being—I have feelings just like anybody else.

MATRON TWO: You did right.

MATRON THREE: Every time something like that's happened, it's always from nerves.

MATRON TWO: It's usually always nerves.

MATRON THREE: These girls all got too many nerves. 'Member one from Birmingham, was wound up all the time? Her eyes just glowed.

MATRON TWO: I remember her—all the girls had crushes on her.

MATRON THREE: Like to scratch each other's eyes out.

MATRON TWO: They was always searching her cell and her body.

MATRON THREE: The Warden was sure she was on something.

MATRON TWO: It was just nerves, just nerves that made her eyes glow like that—but let me tell you, no one wanted to turn their backs on her.

MATRON ONE: Should I call?

MATRON TWO: Honey, it isn't your fault. She'll pull through.

MATRON ONE: I swear I thought she'd stuffed a pillow in her stomach, just to bug me. It didn't look natural the way her belly was spread out like that. She was flat as a board at morning count.

MATRON THREE: Some of these women is just demons—they can think their way into anything. She got herself all worked up just because her mother died. She'll be okay in the morning, mark my words.

MATRON ONE: I didn't hit her. I'm not the type. I'd never lose control like that.

(During the following "nodding" lines, the actors continue the nodding action as an "emblem" throughout the speech.)

MATRON TWO: I was there. You just pushed on her belly to see if it was a pillow.

MATRON ONE: *(Nods)* That's right. That's all I did.

MATRON THREE: *(Nods)* I can just hear the troublemakers now.

MATRON ONE: *(Nods)* That Squaw was standing just round the corner. She's telling the whole population I

hit her in the stomach and that's why she swelled up.
(*Nodding stops*)

MATRON THREE: In the old days they'd have thrown
her in the hole `til she got over agitating. They kept
an Indian in there once til she went blind—didn't give
nobody any trouble after that, you can bet your boots.

MATRON ONE: It's not my fault they won't give her
leave to go to the funeral. I don't make the rules.

MATRON TWO: Just grief made her belly act like that.
My God, she looked eight months pregnant.

MATRON THREE: She was flat as a board this morning.

MATRON TWO: It's just nerves, honey. You did your
job, and you kept yourself in control in front of the rest
of them. That's what you're supposed to do and that's
what you're paid to do.

MATRON ONE: If we took them in our arms every time
they got bad news from home, the whole place would
fall apart.

MATRON THREE: You can bet your boots.

MATRON TWO: You can say that again.

(*They stand at attention, remove their uniform jackets and
transform back into prisoners. All prisoners now "walk"
back and forth from the net to their cells. Some interact
non-verbally asking for tenderness, others maintain
solitude, some look for comfort, a fight, etc. Those they "ask"
comply or resist, but some sort of contact is made. This
contact is always broken when they hear something, think
a guard is approaching or are "caught in the act" and each
continues walking alone until a new contact is made. The
walking continues until RONNIE and EL TORO are in their
cells—then the others move quickly to theirs. CHAMP and
KATHLEEN share the same cell. CHAMP rubs KATHLEEN's
back.*)

EL TORO: *(To* RONNIE *who's transformed into an older woman)* What are you in for?

RONNIE: *(As older woman)* Life.

EL TORO: I mean...charge...?

RONNIE: *(Looks at her a moment)* Oh yeah...murder.

(They freeze. So do OX TAIL, JOCKEY *and* CYNTHIA *who've been listening. Focus shifts to* KATHLEEN *and* CHAMP.)

CHAMP: What are you in for?

KATHLEEN: Bum rap.

CHAMP: Aren't we all?

KATHLEEN: I didn't do anything.

CHAMP: But they caught you at it.

KATHLEEN: I was in the wrong place...

CHAMP: ...at the wrong time...

KATHLEEN: Yeah...

(They freeze. Focus shifts to RONNIE, EL TORO *and* JOCKEY.)

EL TORO: Wow.

JOCKEY: When.

RONNIE: When what?

OX TAIL: When'd ya do it?

RONNIE: Many lives ago.

JOCKEY: Who was it?

RONNIE: A husband of that period.

OX TAIL: Did you do it?

RONNIE: I didn't, but it doesn't matter. I did it a lot in my head, before and since.

(They freeze. Focus shifts to KATHLEEN *and* CHAMP.)

CHAMP: I been watching you.

KATHLEEN: Oh?

CHAMP: Been watching you eat.

KATHLEEN: Yeah?

CHAMP: I like to watch your mouth.

(KATHLEEN *laughs.* CHAMP *stops rubbing*)

CHAMP: You got family?

KATHLEEN: I guess.

CHAMP: *(Pushes her)* Do ya or don't ya?

KATHLEEN: *(Confused)* They're still there, I guess.

CHAMP: *(Starts to get rougher)* Where?

KATHLEEN: *(Moves away)* South Dakota.

CHAMP: *(Shakes KATHLEEN)* How long since you were home?

KATHLEEN: *(Presses herself)* Left at fifteen.

CHAMP: *(Pins her up against wall)* Didn't they try to stop you?

KATHLEEN: *(Stands up to CHAMP)* I didn't give 'em a chance. I ironed all my Dad's shirts and I left.

CHAMP: *(This was the response she wanted—it was a game.)* Far out...I really like the look of you.

KATHLEEN: *(Still confused)* Thanks.

(They freeze. Focus shifts to RONNIE and the others.)

EL TORO: How long you been in the joint?

RONNIE: Sixteen years here. Four in the maximum facility. Eighteen months before that in the county jail. That was the pits. The others were better, but *(Reaches over to stroke JOCKEY)* this one's best of all.

JOCKEY: But you shoulda been paroled by now.

RONNIE: They've been trying to get me out of here all right.

Ox Tail: Were you given a fair hearing?

Ronnie: They granted parole, three times now, but I
refused it.

El Toro: Why? Why? Why? I...I want outa here so bad
I...

Ronnie: I'm innocent.

Jockey: No shit.

Ronnie: Besides, it's safer here than on the streets or
even in my own home.

Jockey: But it's so boring.

*(All fall into images of enormous boredom for a beat. They
change into other images of boredom in time with the
musical introduction. They leave their cells and create one
big "bored" image in front of the cells. Their action during
this "scat" song is to find relief from the boredom of prison—
they act out fantasies of what they'd like to do if free. They
start in front of the cells and move, singing and dancing,
across the whole yard.)*

El Toro, Champ & Ox Tail: *(Sing)*	Jockey & Kathleen: *(Sing)*	Ronnie: *(Sings)*
I'm bored		
	I'm bored	
		I'm bored
I'm sick		
And tired		
I'm sick and		
Tired		
Of being		
Sick		
And tired.		
I'm sick and		
Tired of		
Being sick		
And tired.	Bored	Bored.

I'm so bored		
	Sick!	I'm sick
Sick!		And tired
		I'm tired of
		Bein'
Tired!	Tired!	Tired of bein'
		Sick,
		Tired of bein'
Bored!	Bored!	Sick and tired,
		Tired of bein'
	My	Sick and tired.
	Ass is bored	
	Off.	
That's the problem		My ass is bored
		off.
	The main	
	problem	
Love!	Is—	No stimulation
No stimulation,	No stimulation,	No stimulation.
No stimulation,	No stimulation,	
No stimulation.	Never mind.	Never mind.
	Satisfaction	Satisfaction.
	I'll take	I'll take
		satisfaction
Is there a mind	Stimulation	
Left to rot?		Satisfaction.
Stimulate,	You don't need	Stimulate,
Stimulate	No mind if you	Stimulate,
	got	
	Soul.	Oh oh, Stroke
		my soul
Stimulate the		
Soul inmate.		
	Stimulate,	Fight with me
		baby.
I'll go to the hole.	Stimulate.	
	I'll go with you.	

But
Then they'll put us
In separate holes.   But   But
I'm ready, I'm   Think of the fun   Think of the
                                                fun

Ready, oh yes,   We'll have   We'll have
                           getting   getting
I'm ready!   There.   There.
Stimulate this   Oh please let   Stimulate this
Little old inmate   Me out of here!   Little old
                                               inmate

Flash me a scratch,   Flash me a
                                               scratch,

Flash me a be-bop   Flash me a be-
                                               bop

Up the side of   Up the side of
My head   My head
Flash me a punch   Flash me a
                                               punch.

Flash me a snatch.   Flash me a
                                               snatch.
                                               Flash!

I need it!
Anything!   Flash! Flash!
One more time to   One more time
                                               to

Walk with a flash   Walk with a
                                               flash

On my patch,   On my patch
One more time to   One more time
                                               to

Roll out to freedom   Roll out to
                                               freedom

One more time to   One more time
                                               to

Walk in Jerusalem   Feel the flash of
                                               cash,

One more time,   One more time,
One more time to   One more time
                                          to
Feel the—   Feel the
                                          Cold on my
                                          nose.

And the sun on my
arms
One more time,   One more time,
One more time,   One more time,
                         Oh, I'm ready!
                         Oh, I'm ready!
                         to be
                         An eternal incarcerate
                         Just one more
                         Time, get me
                         flashing,—
                         Just one more time
                         Make me happy to be
                         Walking,
                         Be happy to be walking,
                         Be happy to be walking.
                         Flash!
                         I got the
                         Fascination
                         With stimulation.
                         Flash me a scratch.
                         I got the fascination
                         With the stimulation.
                         Flash me a patch.
                         I got the
                         Fascination with the
                         Stimulation,
                         Fascination with the
                         Stimulation.
                         One more time.
                         One more time.

Flash me a scratch,
Flash me a be-bop,
Up the side
Of my head,
Flash me a punch,
Flash me a snatch.

I need it!
Anything!
One more time
To walk with a

Flash on my patch.

One more time to

Roll out to freedom

One more time to

Walk in Jerusalem.
of
One more time,

One more time

To feel the—

And the sun on

Oh, I'm ready,

Oh, I'm ready,

To be
An eternal

Incarcer-

ate.   Flash!

Just one more
Time to get me
flashing,
Just one more
time

Make me happy
to be
Walking
Be happy to be
walking,
Be happy to be
walking
Flash! I got the

Fascination with
the
Stimulation.
Flash me a
scratch

I got the

Fascination with

Flash me a
scratch,
Flash me a be-
bop
Up the side
Of my head,
Flash me a
punch,
Flash me a
snatch,

Flash! Flash!
One more
time,
Walk with a

Flash on my
patch.
One more time
to

Roll out to
freedom
One more time
to
Feel the flash
cash
One more time,

One more time

To feel the
Cold on my
nose.

	the	
My arms	Stimulation.	
One more time	Flash me a	One more time,
	scratch.	
To walk in	I got the	Walk in
Jerusalem	Fascination with	Jerusalem
	the	
	Stimulation.	
Holding hands	Fascination	Holding hands
With my love	With the	
	stimulation.	With my love.
One more time,	One more time,	One more time,
One more time.	One more time.	One more time.

(All hold. RONNIE *turns to the others, who feel good having played out their fantasies. They sit around. The following scene is a continuation of the scene before the song.)*

RONNIE: Look inside. It isn't boring in here. *(Taps her head)* Nehru wrote twenty-six books in jail. Elizabeth Gurley Flynn wrote a damn good one, too.

EL TORO: Ney—who?

JOCKEY: Are you writing?

RONNIE: Takes too much time away from listening.

JOCKEY: Come again?

RONNIE: *(Grabs* JOCKEY *intimately and slightly rough)* I'd be happy to teach you, if you truly want to learn. I'm a Leo and have dominion over children. I haven't time for kidding or mockery. I'm interested in beauty. *(Looks around, chooses* CYNTHIA, *mainly as a lesson for* JOCKEY*)* I need clear eyes to look into, and beautiful skin to keep me giving. *(To* JOCKEY*)* If you change your dietary habits to improve your looks, I'll consider sharing some discoveries with you. *(Slaps* JOCKEY *playfully but firmly)* If you want to know—really "know" demonstrate this to me by getting hold of yourself and improving your health habits. *(To* KATHLEEN*)* And you, there, you're too short. Hold your torso up, get your head out of your neck. *(Turns and walks toward the cells)*

CHAMP: Christ, she's a Leo, all right.

EL TORO: I'm sorry I talked to her.

KATHLEEN: Do you think she did it?

EL TORO: Who cares?

JOCKEY: *(Dreamily looking after her)* I'm in love.

(Others laugh, call her a masochist, etc.)

(At O M T the following scene was played with physical action juxtaposed to the lines: before saying a line, the actor selects a physical contact activity and imposes it on another. The one "imposed on" has to decide to go along with it or resist. The one "imposing her will" continues the activity until replaced by a stronger will. The action imposed should have no logical connection with the line said. A different will [intention] is imposed with each line.)

*(*KATHLEEN *and* CHAMP *come up behind* JOCKEY, *bring her to the middle of the prison yard.)*

KATHLEEN: What are they putting in our food?

CHAMP: What food?

JOCKEY: That ain't no food, man—where I come from the roaches turn their noses up at it.

KATHLEEN: I'm so tired all the time.

JOCKEY: They mean for us to be.

CHAMP: That's right—they mean for us to be, so's we can't be mean.

JOCKEY: And our pee turns green.

CHAMP: Only thing to do is to quit.

KATHLEEN: I've quit. I can't hold out. I don't want to get out of bed.

CHAMP: You got to quit eating the food.

JOCKEY: They got it all drugged up.

CHAMP: They throwed us in here for drugs, and they's using more on us than the Mafia ever brought across the border.

JOCKEY: You notice Witch-Freak don't talk no more.

CHAMP: I noticed.

KATHLEEN: What'd they do to her?

JOCKEY: They hit her with eight Thorazine. Everytime she looks like she's gonna say somethin', they give her another.

KATHLEEN: I had a Thorazine once, and I didn't wake up for thirty-six hours.

CHAMP: We all got different chemistry. You's a cheap date, baby.

(All laugh.)

KATHLEEN: I don't have the strength to write a letter.

CHAMP: You got a lover on the streets?

KATHLEEN: Yeah, yeah. I know where she is, too.

CHAMP: Do she know where you is?

(CHAMP and JOCKEY look at each other. A slight nod passes between them.)

JOCKEY: She on your list to get mail?

KATHLEEN: I wouldn't do that. I don't want them to know about her.

CHAMP: Where'd you meet? I love love stories.

KATHLEEN: Church picnic.

CHAMP & JOCKEY: *(Laughing)* Oh yeah? Oh yeah? O Wow! What a scene!

KATHLEEN: Well it was. She was from another state. She had a special way of talking. It sounded like singing—but I know she was talking straight to me.

JOCKEY: You got religion?

KATHLEEN: She's my God now—I know no other. It was in the middle of the song I was singing. She was standing beside me, I felt her looking at me, and my voice grew stronger. Then I thought I was getting taller—I looked down at my feet, but I got dizzy. All the people in the audience were looking up at me and they smiled. I turned my head just a bit in the middle of a note, and I caught this blaze in her eyes and I got even stronger. My voice went out to the trees. I handed her the mike. I didn't need it to reach the people. She turned off the mike and held my hand. I sang for an hour, then she helped me from the stage. We went straight to my tent.

JOCKEY: Did you make love?

KATHLEEN: We didn't have to. She was still holding my hand. The light in her eyes nearly blinded me. They were the clearest, lightest blue I've ever seen. Whenever I looked directly at her the heavens opened up behind her head, and rays came from her body-rays that held me up, rays that drew me to her. She didn't know she had these rays… They were invisible. I could feel them as sure as I can feel this floor. l knew I could never fall again. Knew I would never fall. All I would have to do is think about her eyes, and they would always see me—and see her body and she would always hold me.

CHAMP: And that's all you did?

JOCKEY: You didn't make out?

KATHLEEN: Leave me alone. I can't get it together.

JOCKEY: You should get more protein, girl.

KATHLEEN: I thought you said we should quit eating.

JOCKEY: Well, we should probably try it and get our systems cleaned out. But I personally don't think you're strong enough.

(They freeze in the last "will imposed" and begin a section of "walks." JOCKEY crosses to OX TAIL's cell, where twinkle lights blink on.)

OX TAIL: I made a big mistake.

JOCKEY: *(Joins her in cell)* I thought you were gonna play the field from now on.

OX TAIL: I'm stuck.

CHAMP: Do you realize how many times you've been in love in the last two years?

OX TAIL: The more it happens, the harder it hits. I thought you got used to stuff like this.

RONNIE: *(Struts through prison yard to OX TAIL's cell)* The cool like me, we never fall. We let them fall for us. Now me, I got two women working for my validation. Women got to be trained. Can't let them get the upper hand. Even the screws know that. They get out of line, you kick their ass—they'll get down on their knees and kiss your foot. I'm fixing to add another wife soon. You watch how I break the new one in. You do what I do, and you won't feel low down and blue no more. You understand? *(Sings)*
Look around you, hon.
Everywhere y' see
In the prison yard
Or mincing on T V.
You see nothin', hon.
You see nothin', hon.

But a bunch of
Beautiful babes.
Everyone—guarded
By guns.

ALL: *(Sing softly under)*
Hi ya, Betty
Hello Nancy.
Come out Barbara.
Come back Marilyn.
I love Lucy,
Ethel too.
Why don't *you*
Run for
President—Rose?

We're all Babes in the Bighouse,
We're all Babes in the Bighouse,
We're all Babes in the Bighouse,
Trained to love the son of a gun!

RONNIE: So-o-o-o-o-o-o-the
Only the way to go
Is to let nothin' show.
(Others softly repeat "Hello Betty" etc.)
You gotta be cool
If you wanna do
Easy time like me.

ALL: We're all Babes in the Bighouse,
We're all Babes in the Bighouse,
We're all Babes in the Bighouse,
Trained to love the son of a gun!

RONNIE: These women are confused,
Broken and abused,
So how do I show my class—?
I kick 'em in the ass!

ALL: We're all Babes in the Bighouse,
We're all Babes in the Bighouse,

We're all Babes in the Bighouse,
Trained to love the son of a gun!

RONNIE: Follow my simple golden rule.
Show 'em who's boss—
Nobody fools the cool—
Nail her to the cross!

ALL: Babes in the Bighouse,
Babes in the Bighouse,
The bughouse,
The Bighouse—
Hello Babes!
Hello Babes!
(Up you, Mister!
Free my sister!)
We're all Babes in the Bighouse,
Babes! Babes! Babes!

(Lights come up suddenly on the warden's area, in front of the net. EL TORO has transformed into GLORIA SWENSON and is being interrogated by MATRONS ONE and TWO [JOCKEY and CHAMP]. All three face the audience with the MATRONS standing directly behind GLORIA.)

MATRON ONE: At 0-six hundred hours, Gloria Swenson, you were reported by Officer McClannahan on June twelfth *(You may substitute a date closer to performance date)* to be seen in a passionate embrace in the shower with Mary Lou Wiseman. We have rules here, Gloria. This is a very serious offense. Do you have anything to say?

GLORIA: I need another shower.

MATRON TWO: Insolence is also against the rules.

MATRON ONE: Do you wish to compound the charge against you?

GLORIA: I really do need a shower. I haven't been allowed a shower in more than a week.

MATRON TWO: Why not?

GLORIA: Officer McClannahan took my shower privileges away for talking too loud at dinner.

MATRON ONE: You were identified by Officer McClannahan to be in the shower with Mary Lou Wiesman. Is that true?

GLORIA: To quote our beloved ex-President, "I can't recall."

MATRON TWO: *(Snaps* GLORIA's *head around to look her in the eyes)* President who?

MATRON ONE: *(Gives* MATRON TWO *a signal to release* GLORIA, *then smiles and continues in her own style)* Are you a member of that secret cult?

GLORIA: Yes.

MATRON ONE: *(As if she's forgotten)* What's the name of it?

GLORIA: *(Sotto voce)* Jeffersonian Democracy.

MATRON TWO: *(Excited—snaps* GLORIA's *head around again)* What?

GLORIA: Jefferson—...

*(*MATRON ONE *more aggressively signals* MATRON TWO *to leave the interrogation to her.)*

MATRON ONE: *(Sizing up* GLORIA's *"insolence" she holds her around the shoulders)* Looooooooooook, Gloria, we're here to help you. Are you going to cooperate and give your side of the story? Or do we accept Officer McClannahan's report and punish you accordingly?

GLORIA: Officer McClannahan lied.

MATRON ONE: Why would Officer McClannahan lie?

GLORIA: *(Animated)* I don't know. But I do need a shower. Here— *(Lifts her arms)* —smell me.

(MATRONS *move to the right.* MATRON ONE *kneels,*
MATRON TWO *places her chin on* MATRON ONE's *head.*
They drop their jaws, mouths hanging "dumb" in a
"helplessness" image, then take the line from this position.)

MATRONS: That is not ladylike behavior. *(They repeat the*
image.)

GLORIA: Ladies take showers twice a day. You only let
me have a shower once a week. I can't stand my own
smell.

MATRON ONE: *(Moving back to her position behind*
GLORIA*)* When did you stop engaging in homosexual
behavior with Mary Lou Wiseman?

GLORIA: When I stopped beating my husband.

MATRON TWO: *(Pauses—turns* GLORIA's *head, looks*
into her eyes) Look, Gloria, we do not appreciate these
smart remarks. It's going to have to be entered on your
record. Is this the sort of record you want to go before
your parole board?

GLORIA: No ma'am.

(MATRON ONE *gives* MATRON TWO *a sign that she'll*
handle it now.)

MATRON ONE: *(Embracing* GLORIA, *who looks at arms*
around her and laughs to herself) All right, we're getting
somewhere. Now, we want to help you straighten
yourself out and get along here. You want to have a
clean record, don't you?

GLORIA: I want to have a clean record and I want to
have a clean body.

(MATRONS *move to left, repeat "helpless" image in a slightly*
different combination with MATRON TWO *squatting,*
MATRON ONE *on top. They drop their jaws.*)

MATRONS: Put her in Adjustment until she decides to
answer our questions like a rational human being.

(They repeat image, mouths hanging open and maintain this through next speech)

GLORIA: I ain't done anything. You can't put me in the hole for smelling bad. It's your fault. You don't even give hot water. I want some soap. Soap? I haven't been near a shower in more than two weeks. You liars. You ladies. You lady liars. Come out of your closets, you bulldykes, you secret cunt cocksuckers! You're the liars! You're the liars!

MATRON TWO: Take her away.

(MATRON TWO removes her guard coat and becomes JOCKEY again. GLORIA/EL TORO puts on guard coat and transforms into a MATRON. RONNIE, as MATRON ONE, watches the audience as she crosses the space, takes a place on the platform in front of the net. EL TORO, RONNIE and CHAMP impose their wills on one another physically or watch prisoners and audience for trouble as they sing. CYNTHIA, JOCKEY, KATHLEEN, and OX TAIL, in their cells, work on "finding a way out" —they move and step together as they sing.)

MATRONS: *(Sing)* This is occupied territory.

PRISONERS: *(Sing)* We live in occupied territory.
Are you ready to love
Beyond your fingernail?
There is a vast body to behold—
That body is you.

MATRONS: *(Reaching out to prisoners)*
I implore you to swim into the
Mainstream of your own conscious being,
And live in your whole body, too.
Aren't you cramped there, under that
Damp, dirty nail?

PRISONERS: *(To audience. Describing prison life)*
Expand outward into your fist.

Let your mind exist in
Your chest and rise upward to
The tip of your breast.

ALL: Ahhhhhhhh yes, she feels so good—
And you can feel you, if you only would.

(MATRONS move slowly toward prisoners with
outstretched arms. The prisoners are suddenly free—
this is a fantasy section. The cells open,
they crawl out.)

(JOCKEY and KATHLEEN run hand in hand " like youth in
the wood," in and out of the line of MATRONS. OX TAIL
and CYNTHIA sing to each other. MATRONS still sing to the
women.)

ALL: Let me hold your hand,
And you can live here safely in my land.
I won't give anyone your
Phone number,
But you can call me any time—
Night or day—
And we will—

(PRISONERS embrace, MATRONS try to pull them apart—
more "imposing of will.")

ALL: Fling our arms around each other—

(Tug-of war between embracing prisoners and MATRONS
trying to separate them continues.)

ALL: And lay and lay land lay
And lay and lay
And lay.

(CHAMP transforms from MATRON back to herself and
begins scrubbing. RONNIE [as MATRON] pulls KATHLEEN
from JOCKEY's arms and throws her to the floor. KATHLEEN
immediately starts scrubbing toward CHAMP. RONNIE and
EL TORO transform back to prisoners. PRISONERS "walk"
the yards and corridors as CHAMP and KATHLEEN scrub.)

CHAMP: I had a very high standard of living at the Federal Facility. Worked in the laundry and had forty customers a month.

KATHLEEN: How much?

CHAMP: That's a carton of cigarettes per customer.

KATHLEEN: You were rich.

CHAMP: It was real easy time. Some of the women there wanted to look sharp all the time. Know what I mean? And I got paid in cash to starch clothes for the officers.

KATHLEEN: Could you keep it?

(RONNIE *is feeling full of herself—she looks around for a conquest, selects* EL TORO, *approaches her and roughly sends her to the cells to get ready, "walks" and watches to make sure that no one saw her speak to* EL TORO.)

CHAMP: Naw, it added to my account in the Commissary. But I had anything I wanted there. Anything! I never been so poor in my life as I am here.

KATHLEEN: Me too. There isn't a big enough population to build up a really good bank account.

CHAMP: (*Agreeing*) Tell me about it.

(*They continue to scrub.* RONNIE *taps* CHAMP *on the back—a signal that* CHAMP *should be lookout while* RONNIE *"tends to some business."* CHAMP *gleefully runs off to do this.* EL TORO *wait anxiously in* RONNIE's *cell—finally* RONNIE *coolly joins her.*)

RONNIE: (*Not even looking at* EL TORO—*looking out bars*) Lay down on your stomach.

EL TORO: (*Touching* RONNIE) Look, I really like you.

RONNIE: (*Shakes her off*) Hurry—we don't have any time.

EL TORO: I love your nose. You got the same perfect nose as Farrah Fawcett (*Or current pop star*).

RONNIE: *(Forces her down)* No shit! Lay down on this mat.

EL TORO: *(Reaches for her)* I really dig you.

RONNIE: *(Twists her arm)* Then do like I say.

EL TORO: But I want to get to know you. *(Tries to kiss her)*

RONNIE: *(Moves away)* I don't go for mush.

EL TORO: *(Hanging on RONNIE)* It's only a little kiss— what you in for?

RONNIE: *(Forces EL TORO flat onto mat)* For a while.

EL TORO: You're strong.

RONNIE: *(Over EL TORO)* That's right. Turn over.

EL TORO: But I want to look at you. Your face knocks me out.

RONNIE: Take a good look *(Poses)* and turn over.

(EL TORO tries to kiss her some more—RONNIE twists her arm `til she turns over onto her stomach.)

EL TORO: Hey, at least let me take off my clothes.

RONNIE: *(Leaps onto her)* No time.

EL TORO: Oh, please baby, let's undress if we're gonna make love. I'm crazy about you, baby—you send me around the band. Please. Let's take our clothes off.

RONNIE: *(Putting all her weight on EL TORO and beginning to gyrate)* Don't talk. This is the way I do it! I want you to say, "Daddy, my ass is yours."

(EL TORO goes into gales of laugher. RONNIE gets off furious, and shakes her.)

RONNIE: Say it!

EL TORO: *(Laughing some more)* You're a riot!

RONNIE: *(Twisting* EL TORO's *arm higher, pulling her up so both are kneeling)* I told you not to frustrate your Daddy, little Mama, or I'll have to whip you.

EL TORO: You can't be serious. Hey, I dig you, but this isn't any fun.

RONNIE: *(Pushes her down)* If you dig me, *(Crushes her with her weight)* then you'll please me.

EL TORO: *(Cries out)* You're heavy!

RONNIE: *(Begins to gyrate, pumping on* EL TORO's *behind)* O Mama, O Mama. You got a beautiful ass. It's all for me, ain't it, Mama? Give me your ass, Little Mama—give your Daddy your great big beautiful ass. Give it to me. *(Pause)* Say it! *(Pause)* Say it! Say, "Daddy, my ass is yours." *(Pause)* Say it!

EL TORO: You're hurting me.

RONNIE: Say it, Mama—tell me. Tell me what you'll give me. Tell me.

EL TORO: Please, let me go. You're crushing me.

RONNIE: *(Bearing down harder, approaching climax)* Say it!

EL TORO: *(Very flat—to get it over with)* Daddy…my ass…is…yours

RONNIE: *(Reaching climax in sighs and spasms, she cries out)* Oh, Mama… *(Whoops, and climbs the bars as high as she can climb)* I love you!

(Lights come up abruptly on the net area. TERESA *[*KATHLEEN*] is "strapped" into the chair, the* DOCTOR *[*JOCKEY*] talking to her. This action began taking place during previous scene in mime on* RONNIE's *line: "no time,"* JOCKEY *puts on white lab coat and transforms into* DOCTOR, *chooses* CYNTHIA *to help her set up examining room. They cross to the warden's area in front of the net and prepare for a psychiatric examination, setting a large silver armchair with straps on the platform. [In the O M T production, a*

male mannequin dressed as a "pimp" was set behind the chair, his arms placed on the patient's' shoulders instead of straps.] KATHLEEN *has transformed into* TERESA— DOCTOR, [JOCKEY] *directs* CYNTHIA *to bring* TERESA *into the examining room and after she does, dismisses her back to her cell.)*

DOCTOR: You know why you're here, don't you Teresa? Don't you?

TERESA: I didn't start it.

DOCTOR: But you finished it, didn't you, Teresa? Juanita has a broken jaw, and a broken collarbone. She's the fifth woman you've put in the hospital. You fight too much, Teresa. Women should not fight. It isn't ladylike, is it? You lose your femininity when you fight like a man. Don't you, Teresa?

TERESA: *(Under her breath, but audible)* I could knock you on your ass, too.

DOCTOR: No you can't. You're strapped to the table.

TERESA: I promise I won't fight no more.

DOCTOR: You promised that last time.

TERESA: But I promise. It wasn't my fault. I had to protect myself. Juanita started it.

DOCTOR: Did Caroline start it? *(Mock-throws a kiss into the air)* Did Dawn start it? *(Mock-throws another kiss)*

TERESA: I'll be perfect. I won't talk to anyone. You can put me in Adjustment, but please don't give me that shot.

DOCTOR: Oh—*(Pulls out an oversize hypodermic needle)* you remember.

TERESA: *(Trying to pull away)* I'm sorry. I'm really sorry. If I had it to do over again, I'd just hold on to that little shit Juanita until the matron came. I would. I promise

I would. I didn't mean to hurt her—she's just jealous. She fell. She did this to get me here.

DOCTOR: You did this, Teresa. *(Flips* TERESA *around so the side of her bottom is exposed, rubs it with alcohol)* This should remind you not to fight. *(*DOCTOR *backs up, takes aim with hypo and with a big sweeping movement, lands on target)*

TERESA: *(Cries and pleads)* Please don't give it to me. It makes me feel like I'm dying. Please don't…please…

*(*TERESA *begins to shake all over and gasp for breath—this continues throughout* DOCTOR's *speech. The injection is a muscle relaxant—the lung muscles are among those affected, so that involuntary [natural] breathing is made impossible, giving patient the feeling of drowning or suffocating.)*

DOCTOR: *(Removing the needle)* You have to learn to act like a lady, Teresa. You can't throw your fists into the face of anyone who does something you don't like. We can't have a world like that, Teresa. Every time you fight, you're going to get one of these.

DOCTOR: *(Holds up hypo, though* TERESA *by this time is gasping for air)* You must calm yourself, and decide you are going to be a lady *(Moves behind net)* and be good and kind to your fellow inmates and to all the people here who have your best interests at heart. You know, Teresa, we have only your best interests at heart. You have to become a lady so that we can help you.

*(*OX TAIL, CHAMP, CYNTHIA *and* EL TORO *wheel a tray of cosmetics toward* TERESA—*they can work with stewardess images. As* DOCTOR *continues her lecture, prisoners apply eye makeup, rouge, lipstick, spray deodorant, nail polish and perfume to* TERESA's *body.* TERESA *continues to suffer convulsions and gasp for air—prisoners help restrain her when the gasping and convulsions get too great. Audience must be allowed to see that the other prisoners really care for*

TERESA, *but that they must follow orders or they might be in her place next.)*

DOCTOR: You have to keep your dress on and stop walking like a cowboy. You have to start wearing the nice lipstick we allow you. You can make enough money working here to buy the nice lipstick and mascara, and hairspray and perfume you're allowed to wear now. *(Note: After orientation* PRISONERS *are given some makeup privileges.)* You know, in the old days, ladies here weren't even permitted to get dressed up and pretty. But now you can go to the beauty parlor and learn to fix your hair real nice in all the latest man-catching styles. You can get yourself real fixed up here, Teresa. So when you get out, if you shape up, you can get yourself a husband and settle down and live like a normal human being. And raise a family and cook and care for your man and all your little children and be kind to the people who want to help you. You want to do that, don't you, Teresa?

TERESA: *(Through gasps and cries, shaking and flailing, the other* PRISONERS *hold her down)* Holy Mary, Mother of… I'm dying. O Mother Mary, Blessed art thou. O Mother Mary, save me, save me *(Gasp for air)* Hail Mary full of grace. *(Gasp)* Mother, I can't breathe—I'm sick and drowning—take me in your arms. I adore you, Holy Mother.

DOCTOR: *(Calmly in control)* If you promise you'll never fight again and will obey all the rules, and understand we are only here to help you and see you develop in your best interests, *(Spreads arms, opens them to heaven in "Christ's ascension" image)* I-will-save-your-life.

TERESA: Mary will save my life!

DOCTOR: *(Maintaining image)* Mary and I will save your life!

TERESA: Only the Mother of God can do that. (*Gasping and convulsions—goes into fit*)

DOCTOR: (*Leaps out from behind net, slowly approaches* TERESA) You act like the worst kind of criminal male, Teresa! There is a long list of complaints against you! (*Builds and builds till she loses control*) You cut another woman's face with a home-made knife! You stole baby pictures from Johanna! You beat Juanita till she had to go to the hospital! (*Calming herself, regaining control*) If you don't pull yourself together and start to act like a feminine person, you'll get more of these injections.

TERESA: (*Goes into convulsions—other* PRISONERS *restrain her.*) I can't stand it. I'm dying. Hail Mary full of grace.

DOCTOR: Do you promise never to fight again, Teresa?

(TERESA *retches and gasps, the others hold her.*)

DOCTOR: Do you promise to act like a lady?

(*Slowly* TERESA *and other* PRISONERS *nod in unison.*)

DOCTOR: I can't hear you, Teresa. Answer me like a lady.

(*They continue nodding. Others get up and walk like zombies nodding toward their cells.* TERESA *remains in chair, nodding.*)

DOCTOR: Do you promise you will become a feminine person, demure and self-controlled? To smile whenever you see me walk by? To control your temper and learn to walk like a sexy woman? Do you promise, Teresa?

(TERESA *nods.*)

DOCTOR: I can't hear you. Ladies know how to speak.

TERESA: (*Nodding*) I...pro—mise...

(DOCTOR *smiles and injects sedative. Lights dim and come up on* RONNIE's *cell.* TERESA *crawls to cells on her stomach.*)

RONNIE: (*Shouts to the whole prison yard, especially at* CHAMP, CYNTHIA, EL TORO *and* OX TAIL *who are nodding and walking like zombies*) Awwww, you commie prudes give me a pain where a pill can't reach. Why, if we lived in any of them commie countries, we'd be shot or put in jail.

(CHAMP *and others re-enter the present and cross to their cells, no longer zombie-like.*)

CHAMP: Hell, we are in jail.

RONNIE: I mean, we'd be in jail for being gay. Just for that, stupid—'stead of what we are in for. I mean, if I was clean of everything, everything—but just I was gay—they'd shoot me or put me in an insane asylum if I wouldn't go straight.

CHAMP: You'd get proper help.

RONNIE: Goddamn it, that's just what I mean! You think I'm sick! Listen, you nearsighted Marxist. I chose to be gay. I chose a woman to defy the man. It was a political act... (*Raises fist*) ...and... (*Rubs herself on bars*) ...it was a sex act. (*Busts herself up laughing*) Trouble with you guys is, you got zippers on yer pussies, there's padlocks on the zippers, and you have forgot the combination!

CHAMP: You didn't make a political choice—you're just a pitiful victim of a repetition compulsion—

RONNIE: Thank you, Doctor. It's all in my head, so get out of bed! (*A little jivey dance*) It's all in my head so get out of bed! It's all in my head so get out of—

(OX TAIL *enters, transformed into* MATRON, *faces cells from center of yard area.*)

MATRON: Bedtime.

*(Plays "bell sound" violin chord—*PRISONERS *come forward in their cells for the count.)*

JOCKEY: Six.

CHAMP: Twelve.

KATHLEEN: Sixteen.

CYNTHIA: Twenty-nine.

EL TORO: Thirty-one.

RONNIE: Forty.

MATRON: Lock in! *(Rattles chain on cells to signify lockup)* Lights out!

(Blackout)

*(*CYNTHIA *puts on guard coat and transforms into the* WARDEN. *She suspends herself over to one set of scaffold cells to give the god-like quality of looking down on the prisoners. Her voice becomes a tinny drone— by desensualizing the voice she sounds like a loudspeaker. She does not hear the women—nor is she aware of the activity [the passing of contraband] going on inside the cells. The* PRISONERS *hear the* WARDEN's *voice and go about their covert activities, cautiously passing cigarettes, dirty magazines, a vibrator, valium, etc.)*

(The next scene, "Harriet the Snitch" begins as soon as the WARDEN *speaks. Both scenes play simultaneously and can be heard clearly. Visually, the main focus is on the active passing of contraband.)*

WARDEN: Welcome to the Women's State Correctional Facility. There are rules to be followed here. I will give you the daily routine, rules and general procedures of our institution.
5:00 A M. Awake culinary workers
5:30 A M. You will be counted
6:00 A M. Awake entire population to prepare for

breakfast
7:00 A M. Breakfast
7:30 A M. All inmates report to place of work
assignment
8:00 A M. You will be counted
11:30 A M. Dinner
12 noon. You will be counted
12:30 P M. All inmates return to place of work
assignment
3:00 P M. Prepare to return to living spaces
3:30 P M. You will be counted
4:30 P M. Supper
5:30 P M. You will be counted
6:30 P M. Recreation: T V, cards and outside recreation,
weather permitting
7:30 P M. You will be counted
10:00 P M. Lights out
10:30 P M. You will be counted

*(Simultaneously with the above speech, twinkle lights
come up on cells where the women are cautiously passing
contraband.)*

CHAMP: *(Handing a small packet to* CYNTHIA*)* Here's
your Thorazine and Librium. That's a pack.

CYNTHIA: *(Passes a pack of cigarettes to* CHAMP *in
payment)* One pack. Thanks.

KATHLEEN: Stash it all—here comes the snitch!!

*(*JOCKEY *transformed into* HARRIET, *the prison snitch,
enters her cell, smiling and waving to the others.)*

CHAMP: *(To the others)* Watch her. She'll make you
think she wants you for her old man, and then go rat
on you to the screw.

(The women become very busy and ignore HARRIET.*)*

HARRIET: *(Trying to wiggle her way into the conversation)*
Oh Juanita, you have the most beautiful hair. Teresa,
hasn't Juanita the most beautiful hair you ever saw?

OX TAIL: Some have and some haven't.

HARRIET: Who's got a coffin nail? *(Silence)* I'm dying for
a smoke. That movie they had tonight is the squarest
they've had since I been in.

CHAMP: You mean you can tell the difference?

HARRIET: Hey, Dana, baby—I just love to say your real
name, Dana—hey Dana baby, don't get on me, I love
you. I been digging you ever since you arrived—I think
you're neat. I really get off on your attitude—I'd give
anything to be like you.

CHAMP: Some can and some can't.

HARRIET: I mean it, Dana. I even try to copy your walk.

CHAMP: They throw people in the hole for less than
that.

HARRIET: Aww, they're not that bad, Dana. You always
try to make out the staff so mean.

CHAMP: I don't do nothin—they show the world.

HARRIET: *(Laughing)* You break me up.

CHAMP: I didn't notice anything funny. *(To others)* Did
you notice anything funny I said?

KATHLEEN: I didn't notice that you said anything
funny.

HARRIET: Hey, can I have a piece of the action?

OTHER PRISONERS: *(Freezing her out)* Some can and some
can't.

*(PRISONERS fall into images of caged animals. The twinkle
lights blink on and off as the women transform from one
caged image to another. These may be a combination of
still and moving images. Some images may have appeared*

earlier in the play. The WARDEN *never breaks the pattern of her speech. [At O M T it was always about here that the "snitch" scene was completed and the images began.])*

WARDEN: 11:45 P M. You will be counted
2:00 A M. You will be counted
You must keep your blouses buttoned to the top button, keep your collar out. You must eat all food you take at feeding time—all food. You will not make any comment on what goes on in our institution or about another inmate in letters sent out of our institution. You will never use vulgar and/or profane language. Only two people at a time may sit on a bed, and they must be sitting up with both feet on the floor. You may not speak to a visitor without permission. You will not whistle, laugh loudly or talk loud. You will always be neat and clean. You will refrain from combing your hair in the recreation room.

EL TORO: *(Comes to the front of her cell and shouts to the others)* They won't let us have nothing juicy to read!

KATHLEEN: *(Pounding on cell bars, responding to* EL TORO*)* Oh, what I'd give for a hot and nasty R Crumb Comix.

CHAMP: *(At the front of her cell)* Hey, if I had a hot and dirty book to read, you think they would read it with me over the watchdog T V? Or would they come and snatch it away and read it all alone by their lonesomes in the matrons' john?

OX TAIL: *(To the others)* We could share the wealth, but they wouldn't do that, I bet— oh no!

*(*JOCKEY, *as herself again, leaps out of her cell to the center playing area and strips down to her shorts and "coyote" T-shirt. [Whether the actor strips is a directorial choice.])*

JOCKEY: But hey, what if I croon a dirty book to you? They couldn't take it away, hey? No, there'd be

nothing for 'em to confiscate. Nothing to go against
me in my file for the parole board, because it would go
right out into the air.

(*Acts out the "dirty book" story as she "croons" it,
transforming into a pop-art version of the aggressive male.
Simultaneously the others change clothes and transform into
their favorite criminals from the past.*)

JOCKEY: Oh, he sighed as he stared at the juicy melons
straining in their titty-tight circular-stitched Egyptian
cotton bra. Oh, he cried inside his head. Oh, I want to
get my hot and pulsating hands inside her shocking
pink low-cut cleavage, and free those two giant
cantaloupes from their cloth cages. Yes, he husked into
her perfectly carved alabaster ear. Yes, my dewy angel.
Yes, I love you with all my heart and soul. He felt his
member swelling, compelling him toward his goal. He
crushed her shocking-pink -sheathed, hot and heaving
body, and ran his long, hair-matted hands down to the
bottom of her bottom. And his tongue reared up in his
mouth as he gazed upon the outline of her twin love
buttons, pushing forward, begging to escape into his
loving lips. But first he nibbled softly at the base of her
neck. Softly, softly, softly. We got all night together,
angel of my life. I'm going to graze my mouth over the
length and breast of you before I unsheath my own
pink knife.

(*Lights come up on* RONNIE *in her cell dressed as her dream
crook. The others stand behind her in costumes of their
fantasies—the Watergate men, Al Capone, Bonnie, etc.
During* RONNIE's *next speech, the others transform into
specific contemporary criminals and ask, plead or demand to
be pardoned.*)

RONNIE: When my mother
and sisters
find out what you've done   OXTAIL: Pardon me!

to me
they're gonna run all
the way from home,   KATHLEEN: Pardon me!
and tear this concentration   JOCKEY & EL TORO:
camp out by the roots   Pardon me!
and throw it, bars and all,
into the Gulf of Mexico.
They won't let you do this   CYNTHIA: Pardon me!
to me.
My mother loves me.   OXTAIL: Pardon me.
My sisters love me.   EL TORO: Pardon me.
My mother always loved   KATHLEEN & JOCKEY:
me.   Pardon me.
And when she finds out
you took her daughter
away from her,   CYNTHIA: Pardon me!
she's gonna set fire to your
feet, she's gonna set fire to
your liver, she's gonna set
fire to your eyes, and she's
gonna laugh while you   OXTAIL & JOCKEY:
scream for her mercy.   Pardon me.
You can't do this to her
daughter *(Name calling)*
You Jesus-Freak
cocksuckers! You Nazis.
You rusty I-U-D's. You
beer cans. You leaky
diaphragms. You WASP
lickers, you ass-kissers of
he State! *(Pause)* Let me out
of here before my mother   KATHLEEN: Pardon me.
finds out what you're
doing to me.   EL TORO: Pardon me.
This is your last chance.   CYNTHIA: Pardon me.
You're gonna get it, you're
really gonna get it.   OXTAIL: Pardon me.

My mother and my sisters
love me!

(PRISONERS *begin speak-singing "pardon me" from their
cells, each on own dissonant note.*)

JOCKEY: Pardon me!

EL TORO: Pardon me!

ALL: Pardon me!

RONNIE: Oh gee, pardon me.

CHAMP: Oh see Spot. Pardon me.

CYNTHIA & OX TAIL: Oh we saw him—Gerry Ford—
Pardon the bastards.

JOCKEY: I got caught!

ALL: I got caught,
But I wasn't meant to—

EL TORO: They caught the ones in the right spot.

CHAMP & RONNIE: But *they* didn't mean it.

ALL: We all know *they* didn't mean it.

CYNTHIA, KATHLEEN & OX TAIL:
They only had *their* best interests at heart,
And they don't want to be apart
From their wives and daughters.

CHAMP, JOCKEY & RONNIE: They sure as fucking far-out
won't change their spots!

JOCKEY: Pardon me.

EL TORO: Pardon me.

OX TAIL: Pardon me.

CYNTHIA: Pardon me.

RONNIE: You caught me red-handed but I didn't do it!

KATHLEEN: So, you better—

CYNTHIA: Pardon me.

CHAMP: Pardon me.

RONNIE: Pardon me.

ALL: Pardon me! *(Beat)* Pardon me! *(Beat)* Par-don-ME!!!!

(All hold)

(Blackout)

END OF PLAY